100 Ideas for Secondary Teachers:

Supporting Students with Autism

Other titles in the 100 Ideas for Secondary Teachers series

100 Ideas for Secondary Teachers:

Supporting Students with Autism

Claire Bullock

B L O O M S B U R Y

LONDON · OXFORD · NEW YORK · NEW DELHI · SYDNEY

Bloomsbury Education
An imprint of Bloomsbury Publishing Plc

50 Bedford Square
London
WC1B 3DP
UK

1385 Broadway
New York
NY 10018
USA

www.bloomsbury.com

Bloomsbury is a registered trade mark of Bloomsbury Publishing Plc

First published 2016

British Library Cataloguing-in-Publication Data
A catalogue record for this book is available from the British Library.

ISBN:
PB 9781472928467
ePub 9781472928481
ePDF 9781472928474

Library of Congress Cataloging-in-Publication Data
A catalog record for this book is available from the Library of Congress.

10 9 8 7 6 5 4 3 2 1

Typeset by Newgen Knowledge Works (P) Ltd., Chennai, India
Printed and bound by CPI Group (UK) Ltd, Croydon, CR0 4YY

This book is produced using paper that is made from wood grown in managed, sustainable forests. It is natural, renewable and recyclable. The logging and manufacturing processes conform to the environmental regulations of the country of origin.

To view more of our titles please visit www.bloomsbury.com

For Joseph Michael Bullock

Contents

Acknowledgements

I would like to thank all of the students, parents and staff, past and present, at Pembroke School Autism Centre, Pembrokeshire. It has been a privilege working alongside you all these past 13 years.

Thank you also to Peter and Shirley Wilczynski, Richard Bullock, Jennifer Emanuelli and Lucy Evans for the continued support, encouragement and inspiration.

Thanks to Winston's Wish whose resource pack inspired the 'Feelings jar' idea on page 60.

Foreword

Being autistic can be both great and a complete nightmare, sometimes both at the same time.

I got my diagnosis when I was 15. Up until that point I considered myself a failure because I struggled with certain things more than my peers. My diagnosis gave me a reason why I felt so different and so unlocked a whole new way of looking at things, especially when it came to school and learning.

I struggled with extreme anxiety, which often resulted in me leaving lessons, or not even turning up to them at all. I would have full blown panic attacks in the middle of the school corridors. I would often become frustrated and act out, leaving school staff to try and figure out why I had become frustrated in the first place. I would be extremely hard on myself because of my tendency towards perfectionism, and the idea that sometimes things wouldn't turn out as I planned never crossed my mind.

I did have a good group of friends, but I often got confused and annoyed because I couldn't understand certain things that they did or said. Noises and bright lights bothered me more than they did my peers, which would cause my anxiety to sky rocket. I will always remember one day when it had snowed over night, but the school remained open. It was one of the most difficult days for me purely because the white snow made everything brighter and I couldn't cope. My head couldn't process anything because the brightness took over everything. I became overwhelmed and was extremely anxious all day and I didn't get anything done. Another time I became overwhelmed by the feeling of my shoes on my feet (I don't like wearing shoes) so I took them off, but I was already too anxious, and walked round in a circle without shoes on in the playground for about an hour and a half. Simple external factors which most wouldn't even bat an eyelid at could have such a huge impact on my ability to learn.

There were many things that my school did to help me cope better. For example, they stopped me having to go to non-compulsory lessons, and the school counsellor helped me to understand my anxiety and feelings. They tried their best to help me, but there were many other things that would have helped me in school; unfortunately, this book wasn't around at that time.

For example, Idea 3, 'Whole-school approach': if everyone, even the people not directly involved with my support, had been on the same page then maybe I wouldn't have been misunderstood so often. Simple things like using Idea 4, 'Names first', would have helped me in lessons to focus on instructions being given or questions being asked. When it came to lessons, often I couldn't keep up with the teacher, or there was too much information on worksheets and in textbooks. When this happened I quickly became either frustrated or disillusioned, and at that point I couldn't even start any work because I didn't know where to begin. It would take a lot of effort for me to sift through what the teacher had said and what was written down in notes and textbooks, and despite being perfectly capable of doing the work, the whole thing would make me feel like I wasn't good enough or that I was incapable. It wasn't until I reached sixth form that learning became much more of a personal decision, and I could work at my own pace. I quickly became one of the top students in the class. As you will find in this book, it's important that you consider how your teaching methods can be adapted to suit someone with autism.

Had even a handful of these ideas been used during my time in school the whole thing would have been much easier, and I would have achieved what I was capable of achieving. I urge you to consider implementing some of these simple and often costless techniques to support your students with autism. It could make the difference between someone achieving some really great things, or a pupil struggling and missing out on accomplishing what they're capable of.

Mair Elliott, Mental Health Campaigner

Introduction

'. . . the greatest cognitive and academic progress has been achieved by teachers who show an empathic understanding [and] are flexible in their teaching strategies, assessments and expectations.'

(Attwood, 2007)

People with autism experience difficulties with regard to social development, communication and flexibility in thinking and behaviour. The way and extent to which these difficulties manifest themselves will vary from person to person. In addition, many will experience anxiety and sensory concerns. These difficulties can impact on how much the student is able to process, the way in which they learn and the level of support they will require.

This book is aimed at supporting students with autism who go to secondary school. This presupposes that there will be a significant inclusion into the mainstream classroom. However, each student with autism may have quite different support needs and require individualised learning approaches and strategies. No single teaching approach or style will be appropriate for every child. Consideration needs to be given to how the curriculum will be delivered as well as to what is to be taught.

A whole-school approach to supporting those with autism will involve: raising awareness, a flexible attitude towards support and teaching and good staff training. Students will then feel understood and will be able to attend lessons knowing that staff have an awareness of the condition and how it impacts on their individual learning, and support staff will use their shared knowledge of the pupil to ensure that they use strategies in class to help them to learn and cope with the day-to-day pressures of school life.

In a mainstream secondary school, planning and supporting individualised curricula for students with autism, or indeed any Additional Learning Needs (ALN) as well as teaching and supporting the rest of the class, can seem like an impossible task. Taking the time to facilitate a sound transition from primary school into a carefully planned timetable is extremely important. It will allow for familiarity with the school and peer group and remove some uncertainty which will, in turn, ensure increased self-confidence, reduced anxiety, better work output and reduced chance of challenging behaviour. Prevention is better than cure.

It is far easier to build on a solid foundation than trying to 'put out fires' with no structure in place for the necessary support.

Thought needs to be given to how much of the mainstream curriculum students can access and whether or not social, communication and life skills should be prioritised for them as an alternative curriculum. Withdrawal groups can be heavy on resources and staffing but are, for some pupils, essential. It is vital that students feel included and involved with school life as much as they wish or are able. It is up to us, as the professionals guiding them through their education, to ensure that this is well managed. Some will not cope with full timetables; some might appear to cope, but a phone call home may reveal that the student is distraught every evening as they walk through the door. A student with autism will require careful support and their needs must be monitored as they progress through school. They may cope with a full timetable initially, but with approaching examinations, become distressed. We then need to look at how we can help them cope, whether that may be reducing the pressure of a busy timetable or increasing support to make the lessons less stressful.

Students with autism can appear rude, distracted or apathetic regarding work. If a pupil demonstrates these behaviours in your class, then remember they may not realise they are behaving in this way or may not know how else to communicate their frustrations. Think about why they may be behaving in a certain way and how you may be able to help. I nearly always find that if you can help the student feel more in control, whether by increasing structure, trying new support strategies or giving advanced notice of change, he or she will feel less anxious. The less anxious, the calmer their behaviour and the greater the work output. The reverse is also true. Often, outbursts of behaviour are a result of increased anxiety and a sense of lack of control, whether that be as a result of a change to the timetable or a rearranged seating plan.

Students with autism can also be the most engaging, witty and industrious members of the class. Wherever possible, help them to shine by creating a consistency in your teaching, the environment in which you teach and your manner towards them. Paradoxically, you may also need to be flexible in your expectations, your teaching delivery and support systems. Capitalise on their strengths and support their needs sensitively so that their life in school can be a happy and successful one.

The ideas in this book are not exhaustive and will not work for every student. However, they are each tried and tested and have, at some point, worked for a student I have taught. Try some of the ideas — most take little or no time to prepare. Remember that monitoring your use of language, tone of voice or using the student's name before giving instructions takes no time at all but can make a huge difference.

How to use this book

This book includes quick, easy, practical ideas and guidance for you to dip in and out of to help you support the students with autism in your classroom.

Each idea includes:

- A catchy title, easy to refer to and share with your colleagues.
- A quote from a practitioner, parent or child describing their experience that has led to the idea.
- A summary of the idea in bold, making it easy to flick through the book and identify an idea you want to use at a glance.
- A step-by-step guide to implementing the idea.

Each idea also includes one or more of the following:

Teaching tip

Practical tips and advice for how and how not to run the activity or put the idea into practice.

Taking it further

Ideas and advice for how to extend the idea or develop it further.

Bonus idea ★

There are 29 bonus ideas in this book that are extra-exciting, extra-original and extra-interesting.

Share how you use these ideas and find out what other practitioners have done using **#100ideas**.

Good practice

Part 1

Keep this in mind

'Every person with autism has their own character, interests, strengths and needs; the condition does not define them.'

Students with autism can struggle with communication, social interaction and flexibility of thought and behaviour. The extent to which these impact on an individual will vary from pupil to pupil.

When teaching students with autism, keep in mind that difficulties with communication will have a huge impact on their ability to cope in class. They may struggle to process language, articulate responses and understand non-literal language and non-verbal cues. Difficulties with social interaction may mean group work is problematic for them and anxieties around making and keeping friends could be distressing. Students may also struggle with changes to routine and having rigid thinking processes which make it difficult for them to accept new ideas or ways of thinking.

If you have a student with autism in your class, it can be worth reminding yourself of these core areas of difficulty. Remember that even though they appear to be coping on the surface, they may in reality be struggling. If a student is not coping in lessons, their output is reduced or their behaviour challenging, consider the task you have set and whether it is problematic because: it involves social interaction with peers; the students did not understand what was being asked of them; the language used was confusing; too much information was given; or too many changes were expected of a student in a task or series of tasks.

Working towards inclusive practice

'To be fully inclusive, schools need to ensure they are meeting the needs of all students including those with autism.'

Through reviewing our attitudes to inclusion we can ensure that barriers to learning are removed wherever possible, and that appropriate teaching and levels of support are in place so all students are included in curricular learning and in wider school life.

Inclusion strategies for students with autism will vary from person to person, dependent on ability, confidence and need. We need to be mindful that some pupils will be desperate to be included with no 'special treatment' but that, without support, their inclusion would be impossible. Consider the following:

- **The curriculum**: Is it offered to them fully? If not, what are the reasons? Could reasonable adjustments be made?
- **Timetables**: Does school prioritise the learning of life, social and communication skills for students with autism who need that focus?
- **Pupil involvement**: Are their views and opinions sought and listened to? Are they involved in decision-making, target setting and meetings?
- **School ethos and attitude**: Is it positive, proactive and committed to equality at every level?
- **Teaching**: Have staff been adequately trained? Do they use effective support strategies and allow for different learning styles? Is this consistent across the school?
- **Resources**: Does the school make good use of its staff, equipment and time?
- **Exams**: Are access arrangements in place to meet the needs of the student?

> **Teaching Tip**
>
> The school should have an inclusion policy outlining how the needs of learners with autism are met and this should be shared with parents and students. The policy should include: a statement outlining the school's aim for inclusion, reference to legal framework, details of those involved with the inclusion process in school, and links with agencies out of school. There should also be reference to how the curriculum will be tailored to meet students' needs, collaborative working with students and parents, and how and by whom the policy will be reviewed.

Whole-school approach

'Raise awareness across the school to ensure a consistent, whole-school approach.'

A whole-school commitment to including young people with autism will ensure a greater knowledge and understanding of the condition across the school for both staff and students, and will provide a continuous and stable support system.

Ensure your school's approach to supporting students with autism includes the following.

Awareness raising

- Assemblies to educate all students on autism are organised and information leaflets created and handed out.
- Training for all staff is given, including those on school transport, canteen staff and, library staff, as well as teaching and support staff. Core staff working with students with autism may require more detailed training.
- Awareness of sensory difficulties is raised, including how these impact on students, and examples of triggers in and out of the classroom are given.
- Awareness that many young people will experience high levels of anxiety which will require careful support.
- The positive ethos or vision is communicated by senior staff to the whole school and all stakeholders.
- Work with parents and other professionals to share knowledge and information.

An inclusive curriculum

- Students are offered a broad, balanced and, if needed, individualised curriculum.
- Students are at the centre of the planning and reviewing processes.
- Strategies and interventions are used to ensure access to the curriculum is possible.

- Where accessing a subject or task is not possible, alternatives are offered or the time is used proactively to support social or communication needs instead.
- Timetables may need to be flexible or punctuated with sessions where the student is permitted to catch up on work, have calm time or work on specialist programmes.

Consistent working

- All staff working with the student should share information and plan together where appropriate.
- Consistent approaches to sanctions, rewards and strategic input by all staff involved.
- Where a change to an approach or system is unavoidable, the student should be given advanced notice and the reason will need to be explained clearly to them.
- Ensure the school's commitment to inclusion is outlined in an inclusion or ALN policy document.
- Changes to pupil circumstances or concerns relating to behaviour or anxiety should be reported and shared immediately and consistently so that all staff are aware.

> **Bonus Idea**
>
> World Autism Awareness week usually takes place every year around April time. Use this week to carry out a range of awareness-raising activities across school. See www.autism.org.uk for lesson plans, ideas and inspiration.

Names first

'Before anything else, get the student's attention.'

Students with autism may not realise when comments are being directed at them. By using the pupil's name before beginning a conversation or lesson delivery, it is more likely that they will focus on what is being said.

A child with autism often may not listen or focus because they presume that the teacher is addressing someone else or everyone but them. Owing to the myriad of sensory, verbal and non-verbal information that they struggle to process in the classroom, they may drift off task and appear to not be listening.

- Before giving an instruction or starting a conversation, use the student's name: 'Jack, how are you today?' Without first saying the name, the child may not realise they are being addressed and appear to ignore you.
- Be mindful of not singling out the child; try to incorporate the use of their name into the flow of the discussion: 'So, Jack, can you remember what we did last lesson?' Use this technique with other students too: 'Jack, Sarah today we are going to . . .'
- If you notice the student has drifted off task during the discussion or delivery you may need to drop their name into the conversation to help them focus. 'So, let's go over what we have learnt, Jack.'
- Ensure the student with autism is sat where they can hear the teacher and away from distractions.
- Once you have the student's attention, be aware that owing to sensory processing difficulties and other distractions, the child may still need a recap or a hand out, outlining what has been covered in class or instructions that have been given.

Thinking time

'He never answered questions in class or joined in class discussions. I thought he lacked confidence or didn't understand but then I realised he just need a little bit more time to think things through.'

Some students may need a little more time to process language and think through how they want to respond. It may seem that they are unable to answer, and the inclination may be to ask another pupil to avoid pressurising or embarrassing them, but with a little extra time they may be able to formulate a response.

It is important to remember that many children with autism have difficulty with processing language. Additionally, distractions in the classroom, sensory concerns or anxiety can hinder their ability to listen, decode information and respond appropriately. Consider the following:

- Ensure you have the student's attention.
- Ensure any distractions are minimised.
- Avoid speaking too quickly and speak clearly.
- Allow the student a few seconds to process the question – it may help if you consciously count, silently, to five or more before further encouragement is given.
- Repeat the question to allow more time. Do not insist on eye contact.
- Write key questions that will feature in the lesson on the board. This serves as a visual aid which can be useful for learners with autism. You can read it to the whole class and then again to the student. This gives them time and the chance to process information aurally and visually.
- Some students with sensory needs may benefit from having sticky tac, a squeeze ball or something else to squeeze or touch when thinking. It can help soothe anxieties and so allow them to think calmly.

> **Taking it Further**
>
> Introduce 'thinking time' as a whole class strategy. All students are expected to take five to ten seconds to think about their answer before speaking. This promotes more thoughtful, reflective answers from everyone.

Keep it simple

'You will give students a much greater chance of learning and understanding by simplifying your language.'

Some students with autism find processing language difficult. This is not necessarily owing to lack of ability but rather because they have to try to understand what you are saying, put it into context, translate non-verbal cues, cope with distractions and interpret non-literal and 'flowery' language.

You communicate with students, deliver lessons, explain theories and instruct without needing to think too much about it. All students have to piece together the components of what is said, verbally and non-verbally, like a jigsaw puzzle, before they can make sense of this – but whilst most will do so without having to 'think' about it, those with autism may struggle to do so. You can help them understand more quickly and process content more easily by:

- Introducing any new or unusual vocabulary at the start of the lesson
- Avoiding 'flowery', unnecessary language
- Speaking clearly and reiterating any key points
- Avoiding use of non-literal language, jokes, sarcasm and idioms unless you are sure the pupil will understand or you have time to explain
- Avoiding questions or instructions with multiple parts
- Checking students have understood
- Avoiding rhetorical questions
- Remembering that some people with autism struggle to interpret or explain emotions and feelings so language or questions about such matters could cause confusion or be problematic.

Literally speaking

'A student asked his teacher what would happen if he didn't achieve good enough results in his GCSEs. She replied 'Let's cross that bridge when we come to it'. The student looked at her blankly and asked 'What bridge?''

Literal language is clear, unambiguous and direct. In contrast, non-literal language can require some consideration and for pupils with autism, deciphering the meaning can be problematic.

Without thinking about it, we punctuate our conversation with colloquialisms, sarcasm, metaphors and hyperbole. People with autism can have difficulty understanding language in context and often take it literally. As a result, their responses can appear unusual or rude. Sometimes, they can miss the point altogether and not respond at all, even though the comment merits a response.

Ideally, students with autism would be taught how to recognise non-literal language. A pupil in a withdrawal group could work with a support assistant to match picture cards showing the non-literal and literal meanings of idioms. This technique would help him or her to learn how to recognise the difference. This is not always possible though so try to be mindful of the language you use: if the pupil responds rudely or inappropriately, remember to think about what has been asked what kind of language was used. It is also important to remember that a student may appear to understand but this may not be the case. They may learn to recognise jokes or sarcasm when a certain teacher uses them, but may not be able to transfer this understanding to another teacher or another situation. Double check that they understand the use and intention of non-literal language.

Taking it Further

Students with autism do need to learn about non-literal language. Some lessons may lend themselves to teaching about idioms, colloquialisms or jokes. If this kind of language does appear in lessons, highlight it and use it as a teaching opportunity. Visual aids and role play can be a useful way of explaining this further.

Consistency is key

'Consistency in the classroom can go a long way towards helping the student with autism feel at ease.'

In an average school day, a student with autism has to cope with so much unpredictability and change: different teachers with different teaching styles, seating plans, tones of voice and methods of class control. Additionally, they may have to cope with the behaviour of their peers, filter out sensory distractions and get their work done. Many people with autism would simply find this too overwhelming. By bringing as much consistency into your classroom and teaching as possible, you will be increasing predictability which will be immensely reassuring for the student.

Teaching Tip

We all have certain aspects of our day-to-day lives that we like to keep the same. Consistency and familiarity are comforting and reassuring and this is equally true for people with autism. If they feel secure then they will feel in control, and if they feel in control they will feel less anxious. As a result, they will be able to better focus on the lesson and work output will improve. Remember consistency is key.

Taking it Further

The benefits that the above ideas can give are huge. If even some of them could be introduced as a part of a whole-school policy, the school day would be far more predictable and familiar and therefore more manageable for a child with autism.

You cannot and should not keep all aspects of teaching the same, as students with autism need to learn to adapt and other pupils need variation. However, the following ideas suggest effective ways of maintaining some consistency:

- Have a seating plan or permit the child with autism to have a designated seat if they wish.
- Try to keep the general structure of the lesson the same.
- Be consistent in the use of handouts or additional support for the student. If he or she is given a support sheet or you put bullet points on the board in one lesson and it helps, do so in all lessons.
- Be consistent with your method of giving sanctions.
- Try to give homework at the same time each week.
- Keep any trays or equipment in the same place so the student knows where to find them.
- If you have told the students they will be doing a certain piece of work, try to stick to this.

Attention!

'I often see him day dreaming in lessons. I don't think he realises he is doing it – he just drifts off.'

It can be difficult for pupils with autism to remain focused in lessons. You need to ensure you have their attention, but also understand that sometimes this 'drifting off' state can actually be beneficial.

Some students with autism can switch attention between different stimuli, such as focusing on the hum of a computer then watching the branches of the trees moving outside the window. This can result in them being in a very mindful, almost meditative state. It may be that in this state they are still able to listen. One of my students will often seem to glaze over and look beyond the teacher as if he has completely 'zoned out', but when questioned he has heard everything. It may be that the apparent lack of attention is actually because the pupil is trying to process what has been said. The drifting off allows them to filter out other distractions to allow them to think and focus on the lesson.

Some students may struggle to see the point in the lesson or where it fits in to the larger scheme. The topic may not spark their interest or they may be struggling to grasp it. This can also cause them to drift off-task. Ensure you have their attention before you begin talking and briefly outline how the lesson will flow. If the pupil has a special interest use this to engage his or her attention. If possible, allow the pupil to include their special interest in their work at appropriate times. If you can incorporate their interest, you will almost certainly get greater output and higher quality work. Visual teaching aids can also help retain attention and can improve the processing of information.

Teaching Tip

Put a lesson 'map' on the whiteboard, highlighting the key points or tasks of the lesson and the order in which you will tackle them. Draw the students' attention to the board periodically, to show where you are.

Choose your battles

'Ask yourself: is this necessary? Will forcing the issue do more harm than good?'

There are times when we need to help students with autism to understand that they must follow rules, have sanctions and take part in activities like their peers. However, we have to make reasonable adjustments to ensure they are supported and that their needs are met. This can mean that there will be times when making them do as their peers do will not be the right course of action.

Teaching Tip

Incentives can be useful. If the pupil knows they will have extra computer or special interest time they may be more inclined to work with you!

Taking it Further

Work with parents. They are the most powerful tool you have in many cases and they know their child better than anyone. Often, linking with parents can work wonders. Encourage them to explain things at home and support you, perhaps by using incentives or sanctions.

Some students will struggle hugely with crowds and noise and so expecting them to join the school theatre trip or sit through an assembly may be too much for them. If support can be put in to help, such as visiting the room in advance, sitting near the back or going in a little late when the rest of the class have settled then, in time, they may be able to cope. Forcing them if they are not ready could result in outbursts of challenging behaviour or anxiety so it is important to give each different scenario some thought.

Similarly, group work, presentations, sanctions and homework are all areas that can be hugely anxiety inducing for the student. Consider what strategies could be used and which alternatives could be given to begin with, until they adjust to the idea. In time, with advanced warning and some strategic support, students tend to learn to accept and cope but initially you may have to choose your battles.

Visual aids

'Using visual aids and supports in the classroom can help students to gain a clearer understanding of what is being asked of them and what to expect.'

Visual aids are often used in the classroom to enhance or consolidate learning. For the student who struggles to process language or follow what has been said, visual aids can be reassuring and help the learner stay on track.

The whiteboard is now widely used in the classroom. It can be used to display the content of the lesson so the students can see how the lesson will flow – they will know what to expect and be able to monitor the progress of the lesson. Learning objectives, questions or tasks can also be displayed in this way. Tips for using visual aids to support the learner with autism include:

- Ensure any photocopied handouts are clear and the text is not distorted.
- Use highlighter pens or encourage the pupil to do so when identifying themes or highlighting words or quotes.
- If you are using the whiteboard to aid delivery, consider the amount of information on each page and highlight pertinent information as discussed.
- Using interactive games and activities as part of the session can be an excellent way to introduce new material or consolidate earlier work.
- Label equipment to make it easier to find.
- Ensure the student has access to a timetable, colour coded if necessary. This could be kept in their school diary.
- Use lists, calendars, drawings and clocks to help the pupil understand more clearly what is happening or what to expect later that day.

Teaching Tip

If a student is struggling with the pace of lessons or processing what is said you could provide them with schemes of work, handouts or notes in advance so they arrive feeling better able to cope.

Human resources

'Just knowing Mrs Adams is in class makes me feel calmer. She understands me and just seems to know when I need help.'

The role of the Learning Support Assistant (LSA) will be an evolving one. As the curriculum and the students' needs change, so the level and type of support must alter to suit. If you take the time to work with the LSA, listening to their perspective of the student's needs, they can be a hugely valuable resource, saving you time and improving pupil outcomes.

Teaching Tip

Ask the LSA to create a record of strategies that have worked or not, things to avoid, incentives to try, areas of difficulty and special interests. This could be passed on to new staff if the LSA leaves or is off ill.

The LSA can help you to ensure that the necessary adaptations are made to lessons or tasks to ensure the pupil with autism is able to understand and to allow optimal learning. They will get to know the student or students with autism in your class well and will be able to identify learning and support needs. They need to have some autism training to have a clear understanding of how the condition can impact on learning. They can:

- Support the creation of resources or the adaptation and differentiation of task materials, which will help the student keep up with the work
- Support with group work
- Help the pupil stay on task
- Support behavioural and emotional needs
- Feed back to you regarding difficulties or progress.

Taking it Further

Ask all LSAs to keep a brief daily log of anything noteworthy. This can be useful for you to check periodically. If any records are called for in case of complaints or meetings, you have a quick 'go to' reference and it can be a useful way of noticing behaviour patterns.

There is a fine balance between facilitating learning and stifling independence. The aim is to work towards the pupil being an independent learner where possible, bridging any gaps or barriers to learning along the way. LSAs may need encouragement to move around the class if they have been used to working one-to-one.

Parent partnership

'Nobody knows the child better than their parents.'

Parents will be able to provide you with valuable information about their child: what causes them anxiety, what calms them down, how to incentivise them and how best to sanction them. It is worthwhile keeping close links with parents as they can be a valuable source of information.

Strive to develop open and honest communication with parents and ensure they are kept informed of any changes in behaviour, any difficulties the child is experiencing, and their areas of strength. Written reports may not be enough. It is important to take the time to meet with parents if the student is having a difficult time. The parents are with the child out of school. They will be able to troubleshoot possible causes of challenging or changed behaviour that you could only guess at – changes to circumstances, approaching holidays, redecoration of the house or family bereavements could all impact on the pupil and without a communication line back and forth you may not know that these things are happening.

Communication with parents should be sensitive. Reports going home could cause upset. If detentions or sanctions are given, ensure the reason is explained to the parents. Some may appear overly concerned or obstructive, but often they are just anxious. They may have struggled in coming to terms with their child's diagnosis, managing their behaviour and making sure appropriate support is in place. In being open and ensuring regular contact with parents, you will be supporting them and in turn the children themselves.

It's nothing personal

'Inappropriate comments, personal remarks and rude responses.'

Students with autism can struggle to understand how to be socially appropriate, and the awareness of social intricacies and polite behaviour can be difficult for them to grasp. Unable to filter out the inappropriate, they can speak or act in a way that could be perceived as very rude or provoking.

Teaching Tip

If a student is struggling with social awareness, encourage them to: pause, think, speak. This strategy can help draw their attention to any inappropriate remarks or potentially difficult questions. They will become more mindful of what they are saying and will give more considered responses.

An LSA once told me how a student had corrected the class teacher on an inaccurate fact they stated during a lesson. The student was right, and the teacher accepted the correction with good grace and humour. Any embarrassment that the teacher and others in the class felt appeared to go wholly unnoticed by the student with autism. In another scenario, a student with autism who pointed out a 'nasty looking spot' on a friend's face was merely observing a fact, not intending to upset the other pupil and not understanding the embarrassment this could cause.

It is easy to see how during such incidents the student could be perceived as being deliberately rude or pedantic. It is important to help them realise when their remarks are rude, and guide them towards more socially acceptable behaviour. If possible, quietly remind them at the time or talk to them after the lesson. Suggest alternative ways of managing the situation or ask the student to think what they could have done or said instead. Discuss reparation and the different ways they could make amends if they recognise they have spoken or acted inappropriately. Generally, students with autism will not realise that they are saying or acting in a socially inappropriate way. However, there may be times where they have learned that by saying or doing a certain thing, they will receive a certain response. Some pupils may enjoy knowing what the reaction or consequence is going to be for their behaviour. One boy told me he could not resist saying something to a certain teacher because he enjoyed the response (her facial expression, tone of voice) and the fact that he was then, at times, asked to leave the class. In such cases it is important to be consistent with sanctions, keep reprimands calm and perhaps say that you will speak to them at the end of the class when there is no audience. In this one-on-one situation, you will feel calmer and more able to explain clearly why that behaviour is not helpful to you or to them.

Students with autism can struggle to recognise emotions within themselves and others. Empathy and an understanding of how their words and actions can impact others may literally need to be taught. Work can be done on identifying different emotions and recognising signs that others are happy or sad (see some of the ideas in the Behaviour and Anxiety sections later in this book). Provide students with scenarios and get them to recognise the right and wrong way of handling the situation. They need to learn that honesty is a valued virtue in nearly almost all situations, but there are times when answering a question truthfully could offend. However, some students will have learned that dishonesty is bad and honesty good. Their rigid 'black and white' thinking may therefore mean that they will struggle to avoid speaking the truth. In such cases, a good starting point is to teach them to pause and think before speaking. Perhaps they could decide not to say anything if the truth could offend.

Taking it Further

Showing the student a TV clip of someone struggling with social awareness can be a good way of highlighting behaviour that is not ideal, and provides an opportunity to discuss how the situation could have been handled differently.

Transition and change

Part 2

Sharing information

'Make sure you gather all necessary information before the student arrives.'

If a student with autism becomes unsettled in class, there will be a reason why. You will have a far more settled transition process if you have information on what triggers their anxieties and how best to support them.

Early links with a student's primary school can pay dividends. The Additional Learning Needs Coordinator (ALNCo) or designated link staff member should visit the primary school and get to know the new cohort of pupils. A meeting or review should take place up to a year before the transition, with all agencies involved so information can be shared and a plan made for the transition. As a priority, gather information on: triggers, areas of difficulty and key ways to support the student. This information should then be shared with any staff who will work with the pupil, including bus drivers, canteen and library staff. The information gathered can be put into 'pen portraits' – a paragraph or so about the pupil's needs, anxieties, triggers and support strategies. Person-centred plans or one page plans can also be used.

Use the information given to formulate the first IEP and include a target for a successful transition and how staff may be able to help with this. In light of the shared information, consideration will need to be given to any sensory or environmental issues and how they may be remedied. If the student needs an LSA in class how will this be managed? How will they cope with unstructured time such as at the start of the day or break and lunch times?

Transition visits

'The move from primary to secondary school involves huge change. It is essential that students begin preparing for this change as soon as possible.'

Most schools arrange transition visits and make sure that all students in their last year of primary school are familiar with the new secondary school before they start. The student with autism will require considerably more support given the difficulty they may have with transition and changes to routine.

Multiple short transition visits may be required before a child with autism feels at ease. Arrange visits with their Year 6 peers and perhaps some visits independently or with parents. Very anxious students may need a member of support staff to stay with them at all times. Multiple visits may seem like excessive work and planning but it will certainly help them to settle more quickly when September arrives.

Let the student know what to expect from the visits. What will they be doing during their time there? How will they get there? Who will they meet? Be aware that if visiting for the whole day, pupils with autism may struggle with unstructured times, busy corridors and noisy playgrounds. They may need shorter visits where they are exposed to different parts of the day, to prepare them for the full day.

A good way of helping the pupil to express concerns or just to get them thinking about the change is to see if they can think of questions to ask. Ask the Year 6 or link teacher to gather questions from the class to ask secondary school staff or students. This way any anxieties or insecurities can be addressed in an informal way.

Teaching Tip

Let the students look at their new school's website in advance. They could also be given a site map, prospectus and any relevant policies to look at with parents in advance of initial visits. Remember – parents will be anxious too!

Taking it Further

Encourage parents to drive the route to school in advance if this is an area of anxiety for the student. The home to school journey is a daily transition in itself.

Transition activities

'Having planned activities to do on transition visits gave me and the students more structure, and I could tell them in advance what they would be doing the next time they came.'

Help students to understand the school layout, introduce them to key staff and familiarise them with key areas within the building such as the canteen, library and office.

Teaching Tip

Make sure the students know about the school's internal systems, e.g. they need to know where to go if they feel they are being bullied and what is the school's procedure. Likewise, what are the school rules and what should they expect if they or others break them?

Moving to a new, bigger school will present many different sensory challenges. There is the school bell, the larger and noisier canteen, the different sense of space in the classes and playgrounds; there are different rules, different lesson structures and instead of one or two teachers for the day they will have many. This is a huge amount of information to process and cope with given the difficulties they can find with social situations, communication and changes to routine.

During their transition visits, make sure they experience the full school day so that they hear the bell, have lunch in the canteen and spend time in the busy playgrounds. If any areas are an obvious struggle, take note and pass this information on to all of their teachers, the ALNCo, head of year and their tutor. Set them tasks that familiarise them with the school and consolidate what knowledge they have already. They could be asked to use the map to find certain areas such as the science labs and the library or perhaps look at the canteen menu and find a healthy snack they may like to buy.

The first few days

'The experience of the first day in a new school can have a lasting effect on how the week and the term progresses.'

The first day in secondary school can be overwhelming for all children but perhaps more so for those with autism. It is important to use strategies to help the student complete their first day feeling calm, supported and at ease. They will then feel reassured and more in control in the weeks to come. Do not underestimate the value of taking time to help the pupils settle in these early days — it will have lasting effects.

We can all feel a little anxious when trying something new. Often, finding out about what is involved, the time frame or the people who will be present can help us feel a little more in control: we are a little clearer as to what to expect. Over the first few days, help students feel a little more in control by trying the following:

- Give the student two copies of their timetable — one to stick in their diary and one to take home. Ensure the timetable shows the class teacher's name and room number.
- Check in with the student periodically to see how they are coping and that they know where to go and when.
- Consider allocating an LSA to the student for the first week while they get used to the school.
- Ensure the student knows what you expect of them in the lesson. Don't presume they will remember or notice class rules or etiquette.
- If the student's behaviour is challenging or unusual, if at all possible, avoid reprimanding them in front of the class. Quietly point out to them what was not ideal behaviour and suggest what they could do instead.
- Buddy up the student with a responsible friend.

Teaching Tip

Make the timetable more 'visual'. Help the student colour code lessons and break times. Highlight room numbers. This and all of the strategies in the main idea would benefit all children, not just those with autism.

Taking it Further

Give the student a map of the school. Mark on it where their classes are. You could even colour code it to match the timetable.

Getting to know each other

'I really noticed a change when he started to make friends in class. He seemed more relaxed and happy and more focused.'

Relationship development can be difficult for those with autism. They may find the unfamiliar faces and different personalities in their class overwhelming. They will often want to 'fit in' and build friendships but may need a helping hand to do so.

Teaching Tip

Use a lesson or registration session to invite students to anonymously write down questions or concerns to be chosen at random and discussed. This can be reassuring and helpful for all pupils. It can also be a way of discussing a problem or introducing an idea that you want to discuss without the student with autism or their peers knowing it came from you.

Taking it Further

The student may need extra support with social interaction and relationship development training. Supporting them with a) starting, maintaining and ending conversations, b) recognising and understanding gestures and facial expressions and c) knowing how to cope when social interaction does not go to plan, will help the student sustain and improve their relationships.

If you can invest some time in helping students with autism feel comfortable in class and included by their peers, they will settle far more quickly. You can help to remove what can be a huge source of worry for those with autism by helping them forge relationships. There are various ways of helping:

- If possible, place the student in a tutor group with a friend or at least a familiar face from primary school. Check with parents and the primary school whether there are any pupils who would not be suitable, and who their best friends are.
- Acquaint yourself with information about the student: their likes, dislikes and interests. Seat them next to someone with similar interests or a child likely to support and not distract or upset them.
- Carry out some structured 'getting to know you' activities. Encourage students to share facts about their hobbies and interests; this gives those with autism a chance to shine, as they often have in-depth knowledge of their special interests. If they are not comfortable joining in, do not force them to. This could be a written activity if preferred.
- Avoid large group activities, but some paired work can be helpful.

When things don't go to plan

'Help students begin to think about how they will cope when things don't go to plan.'

Life is not straightforward. Unforeseen and unplanned events can occur. You cannot prepare students for every misfortune that comes their way, but you can build their resilience by helping them to learn and think about how to manage difficult situations.

If the student has visited the school and been given maps and timetables, they will have some insight into how the school day will unfold and where they have to go. It is possible that, initially, not everything will run smoothly. Give the student the chance to work through scenarios that could occur in the early weeks and consider how they could manage them. You may need to give examples such as, 'What would you do if you forgot your lunch?' 'Who would you tell if you felt anxious/bullied?' 'What would you do if you could not do your homework?' 'What would you do if you could not find your classroom?' It is important to discuss solutions to these problems to ensure the student is clear on what they could do. Having a named person in a known place to go to as a 'back up' is also a good idea for any worries or uncertainties.

Remember that pupils with autism can struggle with generalising information. They may, for example, know that if they feel that they are being bullied in school that they should tell Mrs X, but if the bullying happens out of school or in a different context, the pupil may not make the link and so not think to tell Mrs X. Incidentally, you can also not presume that the pupil will have a clear understanding of what bullying is in different settings or situations.

Teaching Tip

Write down the scenarios and the solutions, including named staff and rooms so that the pupil can refer to it when such situations arise. If they are anxious, they may not think as clearly and so a visual reminder will be a great help.

Forewarned is forearmed

'Sam went to class and found a note on the door saying the lesson was in the library that day. She could not cope with this. Now we make sure she has plenty of advanced warning.'

Some people with autism struggle with unforeseen events and changes to day-to-day life. The more notice we can give them prior to any changes, the better they will cope.

You cannot give advanced notice of every alteration that will occur in a school day and it is important that students with autism are taught how to cope with change. Remind them of past instances where they have coped and how they could manage when a change happens in the future. Work through scenarios. Help them manage their anxiety (see part 3).

Prepare students for change. Give advanced notice of any changes to seating plans, the layout or appearance of the room, or changes to lesson location, teacher or type of lesson. If you are going to be doing presentations, practical sessions or are changing topics, let the pupil know the lesson beforehand. Suggestions for how best to prepare students are as follows:

- Have a notice board on which any changes are noted. A notice could forewarn of a room change the following day, a school trip next month, or that there will be a new carpet being fitted next week!
- Also use 'oops' buttons or Post-it notes to forewarn of change. Place a note over a square on the timetable or a page in the school diary so that the student can see there will be a change to a lesson, room or teacher.
- Take the time to verbally forewarn the child. Ask the LSA to give reminders or put prompts on the internal register so that tutors can remind students of the change.
- Use the school diary to note any alterations.
- Link with parents if you think that an approaching change will cause anxiety. Phone or email home and ask them to reiterate and remind their child.

Information cards

'These cards take some of the pressure off the student when they are coping with change.'

When facing new challenges or dealing with a change, students may not want to, or be able to, communicate with others. Information cards can be shown as necessary to aid communication and understanding in a variety of situations.

Information cards are small credit card sized pieces of card on which information can be written to help a student to communicate independently in a situation that may be causing them anxiety.

I once made one of these cards for a child going independently to a lesson for the first time. Written on the card was the child's name and the fact that they had autism, which meant that sometimes they struggled to communicate. If they felt anxious at any time they may need to leave the class. The student could show the card to the teacher at a quiet moment at the start of the lesson. Similarly, the card could hold contact information in case of emergencies or if the student got lost.

Information cards can also be used to help the student cope with new tasks and promote independence. The cards could have prompts or task reminders, staff names, questions to ask and information to find out. We have used them when taking students on trips or to cafés to help them feel confident ordering their food independently. Often they do not need it, but knowing it is there reduces anxiety.

Teaching Tip

Use the cards to promote communication between the child and parents or other teachers. The student can use them as prompt cards to help them share information.

Taking it Further

A version of the information card could be stored on a phone to be shown as needed for off-site visits, or for when the student is independent and out of school.

Trips and visits

'Educational visits are a valuable part of a student's school learning experience.'

It is important to include students with autism on educational visits wherever possible. Trips provide great opportunities for the pupil to interact socially and cope with new experiences. As off-site visits are out of the usual routine, preparation is key and can reduce anxieties to ensure the day is successful.

Taking it Further

Before the trip get students to complete a question and answer activity encouraging them to find out about the place they are going to visit. They could make this into an information booklet and share it with others going on the trip. If possible, build your school trip into a lesson plan. Some ideas include: looking at maps, planning routes, calculating distances, researching the location on the Internet or creating artwork based on a theme associated with the place you are visiting.

The amount of support and preparation required will depend on the type and duration of the visit and the individual's needs. Ensure the student and parents have plenty of notice and as much information about the trip as possible. Give consideration to risk assessments, both of the place being visited and relating to the student and discuss any concerns with parents.

To ensure the trip runs smoothly try the following:

- Make contact with the place you will visit and ask when is the quietest time to visit.
- Explain to staff at the place you are visiting that you have a student with autism on the trip and ask if they can think of anything that could pose a problem.
- If possible take the student to visit the location in advance or suggest parents do so. Some pupils will benefit from having a calendar or chart where they can mark off the days leading up to the trip.
- Alternatively you could look at the venue's website, letting the student know this is where they will be visiting, looking at any photos that appear on the website or site maps and discussing any questions they might have.
- Ensure the student knows where they are going, how they will get there, how long the journey will take and who will be going.

- Ensure they have a packed lunch in case they cannot find something that they like to eat and drink at the venue.
- Go over possible scenarios of what to do if: they get lost, feel ill, lose a bag or need the toilet.
- Ensure you have contact numbers for parents. If the student is too anxious to go on the trip or they are risk-assessed for a behaviour that could put them or others at risk, then a parent could be invited to enable the student to take part.
- Create information cards (see Idea 22) for pupils to carry – these hold information that will help them to communicate if anxious. They could be permitted to bring earphones with them if they find travel or sensory issues distressing. Some students may feel less anxious if allowed to have a toy or electronic game with them.
- Ensure rules and boundaries are set before leaving and that the student fully understands them.
- If there are support staff on the trip, sit the student near them or make them aware they can ask the LSA for support if needed.
- Ensure the student knows what to expect from the day. They could be given an itinerary so they understand how the day will unfold.

> **Bonus Idea** ★
>
> Consider pairing up children or inviting a sixth-former or older student along as a 'buddy'. This can help encourage learning opportunities and social interaction whilst ensuring the student is reassured. It may be best to ask the student with autism if they are happy with this first, however.

Getting to and from school

'Whether they walk, get the bus or travel by taxi, what happens on that journey to school can shape the day ahead.'

Many students with autism find the transition from home to school difficult. It can be an emotional wrench leaving the secure home environment and heading off to school where things are far less predictable. If the journey to school is a stressful one, they can arrive anxious and unsettled before the school day has even begun.

Teaching Tip

It is also worth finding out about a student's morning routine before they leave the house. It may be that they need to get up a little earlier or lay their clothes out the night before so that the morning is not such a rush.

Taking it Further

Students could be given travel passports. A note which outlines the route, who the driver is, the cost of the fare, what to do if something unforeseen occurs, who to talk to if they have any concerns about their journey to school or any such relevant information.

If a student with autism is regularly arriving at school in an unsettled mood it could be the journey to school that is causing problems.

If they walk to school: are they leaving early enough to arrive on time? Who do they walk with? Are other pupils or people causing them problems? Do they struggle with sensory issues such as traffic noise, smells or getting clothes wet in the rain? Just talking this through will help. Try to work out solutions such as buddying up with another responsible student who is walking, finding an alternative route or bringing a change of clothes or an umbrella.

Those with autism could find the school bus difficult: the noise, students swapping seats day-to-day, the bus running late, the route or driver changing. Ensure the drivers are familiar with the student's condition and know that the he or she may need support. Students could have a designated seat near the front to save them walking the length of the bus and so they are near to the driver. Bear in mind, however, that some students will not want to be seen to being treated differently, so ask them first.

Moving on

'Moving from school into further education can be an overwhelming and frightening prospect.'

In moving on to college or university, the student will be entering a different and less structured environment. They will have greater independence, free time to manage and many new people to meet. They could also be living away from home. As with all transitions, preparation is key.

The best way to prepare students for this transition is by familiarising them with the new educational provision and supporting them with their independence and organisational skills. They should choose a further education option carefully, keeping in mind the provider's policy and methods of support for those with ALN, proximity to home and course suitability. Enable them to look around the new building, lecture theatres, canteen, library and classrooms. They should have the chance to visit at a quiet time and then at a busier time, to experience a typical day. If at university, they may need to walk the route from accommodation to lecture theatres.

They may also require support with organisational skills. Help them learn strategies to support themselves, e.g. ensuring they have a map, multiple copies of timetables, that they know where to go if they have any concerns and that they plan what to do and where to go during unstructured time. Remind them that calendars, watches and reminders on mobile phones are useful for time keeping. Lecturers and teachers should be made aware of the student's needs and if possible offer course notes, permit Dictaphone recordings and take the time to check the student is coping.

Teaching Tip

If the student has to attend an interview, make sure the interviewer understands his or her needs. They should avoid questions with multiple parts and non-literal language. The student could meet the interviewers and see the interview room in advance to ensure minimal sensory distractions.

Taking it Further

Some students may need guidance regarding personal safety and living alone. Some universities offer mentors who support the student with organisation and independence. A personal timetable to remind them of important daily or weekly chores may help.

Bonus Idea ★

Create a notebook with key information in it: photographs and names of people, contact numbers, reminders of how to manage when difficulties arise etc.

Support for anxiety and behaviour

Part 3

Recognising anxiety

'Most, if not all, students with autism will experience anxiety at some point but may not be able to explain how they feel.'

Students with autism are coping with adolescence, work pressure and new experiences. They will be trying to navigate their way through social relationships, cope with the unpredictability of school and the people within it, and deal with sensory concerns. These are all causes of anxiety.

Teaching Tip

Never presume that just because a student seems to be coping they are completely fine. Look for other signs: changes to behaviour, tiredness, more off task than usual, self-harm, outbursts or withdrawal. Any concerns should be communicated with parents immediately. They will then be aware and can act as needed. Alternatively, they may be able to shed some light as to why the student is behaving in the way they are.

Taking it Further

Ask the pupil to 'check out' of lessons with you, either by using happy and sad face cards or they could just give a thumbs up or down at the end of a lesson.

If you presume every child with autism has anxiety, then it will help you to keep in mind that any changes to behaviour or difficulty with work may have an underlying cause. It will become a habit to 'check in' with the student to see how they are doing. When very anxious the student may display challenging behaviour, or they may appear fine at school but be distressed at home.

One of my students described his anxiety as a physical thing, that when it gets too much it hurts in his bones, his stomach and his head and the only way to stop it is to sleep and so force his mind to stop thinking, or scream and become angry to try and force the feeling away. Some students are unable to recognise their feelings; they know they feel 'wrong' but do not know why or how to help themselves.

Be particularly mindful around exam periods, trips and visits and key events, such as Christmas or the child's birthday. All of these are stressors of sorts and if the student already has low level or significant anxiety, these occasions could prove too much and cause huge problems. We all experience anxiety at some point in our lives, but it really can be unbearable for some students with autism who also may not have the tools or the peer group to support them.

Stress relief

'Make sure the student has opportunities to relax, calm down and release some of the stresses of the day.'

Some events, days or activities may be particular areas of anxiety for students with autism. Build opportunities into the day or week, where pupils can have 'calm time' to help them de-stress and make them better able to manage the stresses of the day.

Make time to find out what makes the student anxious and what calms them. For example, Mondays might be particularly stressful because the transition after the weekend at home is a struggle. Find ways to help ease this area of high stress. The student could spend Monday morning registration in the library to ease them into the day or miss assembly if it is too stressful. Doing this will allow the student to 'let off steam' and in doing so better cope with the school week.

If you know that exercise, time quietly reading, or researching a special interest calms them, then build it into the day or week, whether it is during registration, break times or once a task is finished in class. This will relieve pressure, prevent challenging behaviour and result in greater output. We have to consider this to be a reasonable adjustment and a kindness rather than unfair special treatment. If we know a student is struggling with anxiety then we can be certain this will affect their ability to cope in school and we are obliged to give 'special treatment' to ensure we help them, whether they have autism or not.

Teaching Tip

Remember, even when there appears to be no anxieties, it can be useful to take some time out to relax. Don't wait until crisis point before building this in.

Taking it Further

Add the calming activities to a student's timetable or diary to ensure they remember to help themselves.

Explaining and understanding anxiety

'One student regularly became so stressed and distressed he experienced very physical symptoms that frightened him.'

Experiencing anxiety and panic can be frightening. People with autism can find it difficult to explain their feelings or recognise similar feelings in others. If we can demystify anxiety and help them understand what it is and why it causes us to feel the way we do, we take away some of the fear and help reinstate calm and control.

The following can help to explain anxiety to students with autism:

- Explain that everyone experiences anxiety and stress at some point and that it can affect us all differently.
- Discuss the positives of anxiety. Explain how it helps us to be efficient, work hard and can keep us safe from danger.
- Explain that it is when we have to cope with too much stress at one time or when it gets out of proportion that it can become distressing.
- There are many websites that explain the impact of stress and anxiety on the brain and discuss the benefits of stress and how to recognise when you're not coping. Check the sites out yourself first and then share relevant ones with pupils. One student of mine was experiencing disturbing thoughts, painful joints, tingling and shortness of breath. He thought he was very ill. When I was able to show him a carefully selected website outlining the symptoms of a panic attack you could see the relief run through him as he realised he wasn't badly ill, just very anxious.

Distracting the distracted

'I know when he is anxious. He sits there, lost in thought and he just can't seem to concentrate.'

If a student is anxious then they will be investing a lot of time in worrying about their problem, and this can spiral out of control. Whether in or outside of class, help the student find ways of breaking the cycle of worry and anxiety through distraction.

If you know a student in your class is anxious then there are several ways you can help to ease them out of their internal world of worry and get them mentally back into the class, able to learn:

- Talk to the child about their anxieties. If they are unable or unwilling to talk, ask colleagues if they know of the cause of anxiety.
- Keep the lesson and communication with the child as straightforward and predictable as possible to avoid adding to the anxiety.
- Keep them on task. It is impossible to think of two things simultaneously. You cannot worry about tomorrow's school trip at exactly the same time you are trying to solve an equation.
- Keep them busy. When one task is completed, ensure they have another one to start.
- Use special interests as part of the lesson or as an incentive to complete work.
- Pictures of something to do with the special interest or something that makes the student smile can be useful. Stick them in their diary. This worked brilliantly for a student of mine whose special interest was tigers. When anxious, he would flick to the picture, calm himself down and resume the task.
- Having some sticky tack, a small toy or a rubber can help distract and calm the student.

Teaching Tip

Students with autism can struggle with unstructured time, and if they have finished their task they may begin the cycle of worry again. Encourage them to complete the task and then keep them busy by asking them to help you give out or collect books, tidy up or go on a message errand.

Self help

'One student was regularly missing classes owing to anxiety.'

There has been an increase in the use of mindfulness as a whole-school approach and results are very encouraging. By teaching students how to calm themselves down, we are helping them feel in control and better able to cope with life's stresses.

The whole class could benefit from these simple ideas. They need only be taught once and then the students have a tool for life that can be completed at any time. I have seen remarkable transformations in children who have learned to build calming tools into their day-to-day lives.

- Make the out breath longer than the in breath. Breathe in for five and out for nine, or in for seven and out for 11. This longer out breath signals to the brain you are calm, even if you aren't!
- When stressed we tend to take shallow, quick breaths. Make your breath deeper, filling your abdomen with air.
- Practice mindfulness. Focus completely on one thing, study it. This could be simply noticing how your body feels, scanning each part as you move from head to toe. Alternatively, focus intently on the desk in front of you, the material, texture, any marks and how it feels to touch. If you are thinking of that, you cannot be thinking of a worry at the same time. If the mind wanders, return to the point of focus.
- Encourage students to write their worry down and postpone worrying for a time. The act of writing it down but knowing they are not dismissing it and can return to it later when calmer can help.

Get physical

'Exercise is one of the most powerful ways to reduce anxiety.'

Research studies have shown that regular exercise benefits students with autism. It can help reduce anxiety, aggression and challenging behaviour and aid sleep. It can also help reduce stimulatory behaviours that some students with autism may display such as flapping, tapping or rocking.

It may be difficult to fit regular exercise into the mainstream secondary school timetable but at the very least it should be encouraged. Several of our students benefited hugely from regular use of the multi gym and the local leisure centre. PE lessons will be on the timetable, but it may be that those with autism cannot cope with group or contact sports; in this case, alternative exercise sessions should be put in place. Running during lunch times could be encouraged.

Also encourage students to exercise regularly out of school. Work with parents. We all know the scientifically proven benefits of exercise; we need to encourage this for children with autism out of school. If it is a struggle to engage them in more typical forms of exercise classes then try the trampoline, cycling, running in the park or sports with clear rules and structure such as martial arts. Many of our students have taken karate and this has kept them fitter and calmer but also taught discipline and control.

Whilst this may be difficult to put in place, the lasting impact of regular exercise can carry over into the classroom and have a huge impact on behaviour and attention.

Teaching Tip

For students with severe anxiety, rather than withdrawal time and crisis management, build regular exercise into the timetable and Individual Education Plan (IEP) if possible.

One-to-one worry work

'*Sometimes the students will need some one-to-one support to help them through anxious times.*'

If a student is increasingly anxious and it is impacting on school, then additional support may be required. Sometimes, sitting down one-to-one with a person they trust can help.

Teaching Tip

There are many great workbooks available to work through with students experiencing anxiety. Your local health board or Child and Adolescent Mental Health Service (CAMHS) should have resources.

Taking it Further

If the problem continues or worsens, the student may need a referral to an external agency such as CAMHS, or alternative psychological or emotional health team.

The aim is to help the student identify the cause of their anxiety and establish a way forward.

- Help them to identify what is a real concern and what has grown out of proportion. Remember not to belittle the student's worry. What can seem absurd to us can be terrifying for them.
- Identify which worries we can do something about and which we cannot. Where something can be done, such as planning a revision timetable to reduce exam stress, do it. If nothing can be done, such as worrying about a meteor crashing to earth, then reassure, help them see a realistic perspective and encourage them to write the worry down and let it go.
- Remind them worry is just thoughts out of control and that they can choose a better thought. Encourage them to think about the positives in their life: good family relationships, exercise, healthy eating, being on top of school work, friends and security. If one of these is lacking, they may need additional help.
- If they cannot identify what is making them anxious, then write down a list of what they were doing before the panic began to help put the pieces of the puzzle together. They can also build up a diary of how they helped themselves to feel better, for future reference.

Reassuring reading

'The script reassures Joe and reminds him how he can help himself. Just reading it calms him down.'

Affirmations are positive statements that can be read or repeated silently to reassure and calm. Similarly, scripts or a few lines of writing can be produced for the student to read at times of distress. One pupil chose to carry his on a credit card sized piece of laminated paper in his wallet so he had it with him at all times.

Helping the pupil write a positive message for themselves can be a helpful way to reframe negative thoughts and remind them of helpful strategies. A brief positive statement such as 'I am happy and relaxed and breathing calmly' could be noted down or repeated. Slightly longer scripts could be written in the first person out lining the anxiety, reassurance and how to support themselves.

A student who doesn't like crowds, for example, could have a script saying 'I do not like crowds. I do not like the noise or people pushing past. When I feel like this I can remember that I am safe and there are people who can help me. I will feel better if I breathe calmly, leave for lessons a little earlier and go to the library for some quiet time.'

'Social stories', developed by Carol Gray, are a more detailed and prescriptive way of writing these type of scripts and have been highly effective for many students. She has written many books, and examples are also given on her website: www.carolgraysocialstories.com.

> **Taking it Further**
>
> Involve parents and encourage the students to keep a copy of their script at home. The more this kind of writing is reinforced the better.

Coping with mistakes

'Everything has to be perfect.'

When the outcome of a task does not go to plan, students with autism can get very distressed. A mistake is effectively an outcome that they did not predict or plan for. Students can be supported in coping with mistakes and managing their emotional responses when they occur.

Given their rigid thinking and a dislike of the unpredictable, it is clear why making mistakes can cause such anxiety for some people with autism. As a result, some students can spend a long time on a piece of work, determined to achieve a perfect end result. This can result in their not finishing the work, and a sense of not having completed the work as planned can cause huge distress. One student used to write beautifully, but he would have to ensure the script was perfect and would go over every letter to ensure the ink was deep enough and an even colour. Every piece of writing took an age. Some students will become so distressed at not achieving their desired outcome, grade or standard of work that they will be unable to cope and will struggle to articulate their distress. Challenging behaviour and emotional outbursts may occur as a consequence.

The following can help students cope with making mistakes or running out of time to complete their work:

- Reassure the student that everyone makes mistakes and that it is through mistakes that we learn best. Many of the most famous and revered scientists, artists, explorers and inventors made mistakes and 'got it wrong' before attaining success.
- Show the student good work they have achieved and progress they have made.

- Allow plenty of time for tasks and use verbal reminders and timers to help the student keep track of time.
- Use scenario cards to work through what to do if they make a mistake. This could include mistakes socially as well as with work. How could they manage such situations?
- Create a 'social story'. This is a great way of highlighting that everyone makes mistakes, giving reassurance and providing a solution. See Carol Gray's website: www. carolgraysocialstories.com.
- Make 'Oops' or 'No problem' cards for students to consult to remind them of strategies to stay calm.
- Some students will be unable to move on if a mistake has been made. Reduce stress by using a computer or pencil rather than a pen, in order to make amendments easier and less obvious.
- Sometimes the student will need a little time to calm down. When their frustration subsides, they may be able to cope with distraction or being encouraged onto the next step or task.

> **Bonus Idea**
>
> Extra time tokens. These can be used when the student is running out of time and getting distressed. They can be handed to the teacher in exchange for extra time to complete a task or assignment.

Girls

'I had no idea she had autism – she has friends and has no trouble communicating!'

Girls with autism may cope differently to boys with the condition, both in social situations and with relationship development. It is important to be aware of these differences and that, at times, autism in girls may be more difficult to identify.

If a female student with autism is able and quietly hard working, then it could be easy for her condition to go undetected. In addition, many are quite able to chat with peers, are affectionate and manage to interact socially and so appear to be coping well. Their female peers may be accepting of slight awkwardness or differences and so they can be a part of a social group. Of course, this is not the case for all students, but it explains how some girls appear not to have any support needs.

Although they may seem to be coping well, some girls will struggle to keep up with the fast paced and ever evolving world of the adolescent female. Magazines, films and social media may not interest them but are an increasingly important part of their friends' lives. They may struggle with going out with friends to different places, with different people and not feel ready to explore the new experiences of dating, wearing make-up, drinking or staying over at friends' houses. All of this can make them feel isolated. They will need support keeping themselves safe as they are potentially more vulnerable than their peers. Having a supportive adult with whom they can share fears or concerns is important. External agencies may need to be called upon, particularly if the girl is experiencing depression or anxiety.

Anxiety support kit

'This practical strategy gets the student thinking about their anxiety and provides them with tools to help them during difficult times.'

The support kit or toolbox allows students to create and discover ways to help themselves during times of anxiety. It is a go-to resource as and when needed and various versions could be made to suit different individual needs, personalities and settings.

This activity could be done as a whole class task or with individuals. Encourage students to talk about the things that make them happy or that they find relaxing. Begin by noting some of these ideas down. The support kit can be completed simply in paper format. Students can list the things they will do when they feel anxious and keep the list as a reminder. You may like to use a worksheet with the outline of a tool box or first aid kit with different shaped tools or boxes and bottles on it. The students write an idea on each, colour it in and personalise it. Ideas could include: read a book, go for a run, do a special interest, look at a distraction card, read a script or 'social story', meditate, have a bath.

Alternatively, you can use a shoebox or plastic container and actually fill the box with the tools identified. The student could keep a copy of the cards, the script, a favourite book, picture or small game, colouring book, notepad, a copy of a favourite DVD or a treat snack. Some of these items could be kept in an envelope, be stuck in diaries or made into a small booklet; whatever suits the individual. What is important is that on opening the box or looking at their list or booklet, the student is instantly faced with positive ideas and reminders of how to help themselves.

Teaching Tip

The support kit and its contents can evolve as the student's needs and interests vary. As the student gets older, anxieties may change and the contents of the box will need to be altered to support this.

Taking it Further

This idea can be used for specific worries such as approaching exams or school trips. Tailor the tools to suit the need. If the student is going on a school trip, for example, then the social story would be tailored to fit this and the kit may include a favourite toy/ game, snack and a copy of the day's itinerary.

Student voice

'Ten things students with autism wish you knew.'

Over the years I have asked students with autism what they would tell teaching staff about autism if they could. Every time the answers are very similar, and if every teacher took these points on board it would make a big difference.

Teaching Tip

Gather students' ideas and make leaflets of your own or use the ideas listed in this chapter.

The idea of isolating main areas of concern for students with autism came from the title of a book *Ten Things Every Child with Autism Wishes You Knew* by Ellen Notbohm. During a pupil council meeting one year, I gathered my students' views and made them into leaflets to hand out to staff. The leaflets were more detailed, but the main ideas are outlined here:

- Please try not to use confusing language.
- Please keep instructions clear, sometimes we get told off for not listening.
- We are all different, autism is a spectrum condition.
- Some people with autism find changes to routine difficult to cope with.
- Some of us have sensory difficulties.
- If we have done something wrong please explain it to us calmly.
- Some of us find it difficult to talk about emotions or understand how other people are feeling.
- It can really help some of us to have something visual to help us to understand.
- Some of us get bullied and wound up. Sometimes we are asked to work in groups with these people. This is really hard for us.
- Sometimes we leave class early to get to the canteen or to get home. Some supply teachers won't let us leave early, even when we tell them, and this can be upsetting.

Taking it Further

Make a leaflet about what students with autism would like their peers to know. Tutors could hand these out to all the students in their form.

Behaviour

Part 4

Detective work

'There is always a reason for challenging behaviour. The first step is trying to establish what that may be!'

It is worth spending a little time trying to identify what may be the trigger or cause of challenging behaviour for children with autism. Do not underestimate how the following could impact on a student and their behaviour, and how supporting them could make your life in the classroom a lot calmer. Remember the student may not be able to tell you what is wrong.

Initially it is worth considering the different reasons for the behaviour. Could the student be:

- Struggling to communicate their feelings, thoughts, needs, answers?
- Unable to process what is being said or taught?
- Bored? Is the lesson content too difficult, easy or of no interest to them?
- Unwell or anxious?
- Struggling with change or transition at home or school? Does the behaviour happen at the start/end of lessons?
- Finding unstructured time or group work difficult?
- Struggling with sensory difficulties?
- Wanting more – or less attention – in class?

Work through the above as a check list. If you can identify one or more areas as problematic, then think how this may be addressed and read on for extra support ideas.

Physical challenge

'Sometimes words are not enough and students express their frustration physically.'

Physical outbursts in the classroom are distressing. There are some strategies that can help to prevent a situation from escalating and calm the student down, or at least reassure you that you tried your best to diffuse the situation whatever the outcome.

If a student is a little unsettled, kicking at a chair, knocking books to the floor or refusing to speak or engage, then these initial signals need to be addressed, although it may be possible that you have no option but to let the behaviour run its course. If the behaviour is putting the student or others at risk or the disruption is unmanageable, the following could help prevent escalation:

- Encourage the student to leave the classroom and move to a quieter space.
- If they will not move, request that the other students leave and wait outside. Ask one of these pupils to get help.
- Try to distract the student. Talk about interests, yourself, pets – anything that will help the pupil stop giving energy to the negative thoughts. If you are unsure of the trigger, avoid potential flashpoints such as family, friends or work.
- You will know the students. If they respond to humour, try that.
- Encourage calm breathing, offer reassurance and remain in a calm stance, keeping your voice as even as possible.
- It may be useful for another staff member to take over and for you to step back. Sometimes a different approach, tone of voice or face can trigger a change in behaviour.

Teaching Tip

Try to discern what the trigger for the behaviour is. Has the task been understood? Was the content of the lesson upsetting for some reason? It is also important to talk with the student afterwards and find out what triggered the behaviour and what, if anything, can be done to prevent a reoccurrence (see Idea 41). A physical outburst can be frightening or worrying to see. Record the incident carefully and talk it through with a colleague afterwards. Look after yourself during and after the incident.

To sanction or not to sanction

'We are told that she needs to have sanctions for her behaviour like the other students, but we are also reminded that she has autism and we should to take that into account! Where does that leave us?'

Students need to learn that there are rules and consequences when the rules are broken, but not at any cost. Look at each individual, decide how you will manage their behaviour with them and their parents so that they all are aware . . . and then stick to it!

If the student has an IEP, it should clearly state the strategies to motivate good behaviour, but should also refer to any sanction that may be put in place and why this may be. The IEP can be used to track and monitor the success of behaviour support strategies.

Many students with autism will want to be treated like their peers and will be able to cope with sanctions. Some will find this genuinely very difficult to manage. Their peers may feel changes to sanctions for students with ALN are unfair, but there will be times where this will have to happen; they have a diagnosis of a condition which means they have needs that are different from their peers. Educational support will, at times, need to be tweaked in acknowledgment of this.

An example of a misjudged sanction is as follows. Much work went into reducing anxiety and supporting a Year 7 pupil. A physical outburst resulted in a temporary exclusion. The child was devastated but accepted the sanction. The following week he was expected to miss a school trip as he had been excluded. He had been punished for his outburst and now, a week later he was, as he saw it, being punished again. Anxiety increased, behaviour deteriorated and attendance dropped.
Ensure the student and parents understand the implications of sanctions and the wider behavioural policy. If the result of imposing heavy sanctions is likely to distress the student, cause anxiety and create huge problems for them, then question whether it is the best course of action.

When sanctioning a student with autism, think about the following:

- Make sure the student and parent understand the sanctions and when or for what reason they are being given.
- Be consistent in your reasons for giving the sanction. Consider if a sanction is necessary or, if using motivators, whether an explanation and strategies to support behaviour would allow a better outcome for a person with autism.
- Some may not be able to link what happened last week with this week's detention. They are more likely to comply, learn from the sanction and cope with this change to routine if it is carried out that day.
- Students with autism tend to prefer sticking to rules if they understand the reasoning behind them. Talk with them. Do they realise their behaviour is having such an impact? Some do not.
- Where possible, use positive reinforcement and rewards to encourage positive behaviour.
- If a student is repeatedly behaving in a certain way and receiving sanctions, they may not be fully understanding of how their behaviour is linked to the sanction. Alternatively, they may not know how to manage their behaviour in that circumstance. Staff may need to consider whether the sanction is appropriate.

> **Bonus Idea** ★
>
> Give parents and students a copy of the school's behaviour policy. If you have special arrangements for a child, keep a written copy for yourself and share with parents.

Debriefing

'This strategy can help prevent similar incidents occurring in the future.'

Following an instance of challenging behaviour, it is very useful to discuss the incident with the student. In finding out the cause, talking about what happened and thinking how this could have been better managed, you will be helping the student to cope should a similar situation occur in the future.

This process is useful and if used consistently can help students understand and manage their own behaviour. It is important to remember that children with autism may respond differently from their peers when questioned or asked for an explanation. They may struggle to explain feelings or how or why they acted as they did. They may appear to show no empathy or sympathy for others involved and fail to understand why they are in trouble, perceiving their actions as justified. This can be difficult to manage, particularly if the student refuses to acknowledge any fault. When calm, speak with the student.

- Find out what caused the behaviour if possible; this could be a chain of events.
- Allow the student to calm down, but ideally talk with them on the day of the incident. Some students will arrive the next day calm and expecting a fresh start and so to begin talking about yesterday's incident could cause distress or a return to anxious or challenging behaviour.
- If appropriate, ask all parties involved to give their version of events. It may be easier to get written accounts. It can be difficult for peers to see no remorse or admission of blame from the student with autism.
- Discuss what happened and encourage everyone involved to think about where

things got out of control. It may be useful to explain that people will have different perceptions of what happened but that whatever the cause, the behaviour was not acceptable.

- Consider alternative ways the student could have managed the situation. Set out a plan, introduce strategies and offer support. At what point could they have acted differently?

This may not be the first incident of its kind. Draw the student's attention to this and explain similarities between this situation and previous incidents. Remind them of how they agreed to handle the situation previously. People with autism cannot always transfer skills, so they may not be able to instantly draw on previous experiences – you may need to go over this several times after several similar incidents.

Bonus Idea ★

Go through some scenarios with the pupil and get them to record how they could correctly handle such situations without resorting to challenging behaviour. Role playing scenarios could also be useful, and could form part of a social skills group.

Challenge checklist

'Sometimes students are constantly challenging and there seems to be no identifiable reason.'

There is always a reason for challenging behaviour, but when there is no obvious cause for repeated incidents or when the student will not or cannot alter their behaviour, accommodating them in the classroom can become very difficult. A challenge checklist provides a useful overview and can enable staff to identify which areas to focus on.

To remind me of what needs to be tried in complex cases where there seems to be no easy solution, I keep a checklist which prompts me to:

- Get brief reports from all staff on behaviour and work output to see if any patterns emerge.
- Check the behaviour record: are sanctions consistent and are there any patterns?
- Ensure all staff are aware of the child's needs and autism-friendly teaching strategies.
- Talk to the child: do they realise their behaviour is unacceptable, do they know why, and do they understand the ultimate consequences?
- Contact parents to check how behaviour is at home, if there have been any changes, and to discuss concerns or get advice.
- Consider whether the student has a named person or place to go to when they are distressed.
- Check if there is any external agency involvement.

Alongside the checklist, keep a record of all correspondence, phone calls, strategies tried and reports. If the student needs to move to another provision or a paediatrician needs information, providing these materials will ensure appropriate care and will demonstrate careful monitoring and tracking on behalf of the school.

Talk time cards

'He is so desperate to talk about his special interest he continually interrupts the lesson.'

Some people with autism will find it very difficult to stop themselves sharing their thoughts or observations. At times this is fine and should be encouraged, but there will be times where this is not ideal and can disrupt the lesson. Talk time cards allow the teacher to continue with the lesson whilst reassuring the student they will be listened to.

This is a simple but very effective idea that I have used often. One student talked at length about dinosaurs, his special interest. Limited response was required from those addressed, but he expected everyone to listen. We introduced a card titled 'talk time'. A talk time card has a box for the student to complete, saying 'teacher's name' and underneath: 'I would like to talk about . . .' and space for the child to write a line or two. This is then given to the teacher who will agree a time to discuss what was written on the card.

Talk time cards give the teacher the opportunity to delay the conversation until a more suitable time, yet give the student with autism the reassurance that they will get their chance to share their thoughts. Talk to the student about the strategy, making sure they understand that there is a limit of one or two points per card, one or two cards per lesson and also set a time limit for the 'talk time' session. The students for whom this would be beneficial but who would be self-conscious about using the card could note the points down in their diaries or a notebook.

Teaching Tip

Talk time cards could be used as a whole-class strategy in tutor groups where concerns or queries are posted in a box or tray to be addressed daily or weekly.

Bonus Idea ★

Use the same idea for students who want to share information or have a concern, in or out of the classroom.

Time out

'This gives the student a way out when they are unable to cope.'

These cards can be used by the student when they are unable to cope or feel that they will not be able to manage their behaviour. Rather than staying in class and getting gradually more unsettled, they can remove themselves before an outburst occurs.

Teaching Tip

Remember to let supply or new staff know about the strategy. If the student relies on this strategy and is reassured that they can use it to calm their anxiety then it must be used consistently. If staff fail to use it correctly, the student could become very distressed and the strategy may not work in the future.

Taking it Further

Teachers could use a time out card or suggest time out to the student, if there are signs they are not coping.

Students with autism may benefit from being permitted to have time out of the classroom when feeling anxious or angry. At times, simply knowing this option is there can be enough. Students seldom manipulate this strategy, tending only to use it when really needed. That said, there will be some pupils who you will know would enjoy using this far too often, and for them it may not work!

The time out can be requested by the child verbally. Alternatively, if students are unable to verbalise the request because they are to distressed or would rather be less conspicuous, a card could be used. The time out could be a few minutes in the corridor, going to the library or to a named person and place. Make sure the procedure of where, for how long and to whom the student goes is established and made clear to all involved. This has worked wonders for students who need to start working on emotional regulation and recognising when they are beginning to struggle. It helps them manage their own behaviour. The next step is finding and using strategies so it does not get to this point, but this is a great starting point.

It is vital all staff teaching the student are made aware of the strategy and what is and is not permitted so it is used consistently.

Identifying emotions

'Students with autism may need help recognising their emotions.'

Students with autism can struggle to understand why they are feeling a certain way or recognise emotions in others. If we can help them understand how they feel and why this may be, they will be better able to regulate their behaviour and responses to stress.

Students may experience physical sensations such as fluttering in the stomach and heat in the cheeks, but they may not attribute this to nervousness. They may note their rapid heartbeat, churning stomach and shallow breathing, but not realise they are experiencing anxiety. If you suspect this is the case, the student will need some help in learning to recognise some of the different emotions.

If possible, social skills groups or one-to-one sessions for a short period could focus on this. It may mean temporary withdrawal from a mainstream subject, but if they can grasp this, they will be able to recognise when they are feeling a certain way and employ strategies to help themselves. This will prevent outbursts in the classroom. These sessions could explore:

- What are different emotions?
- When do we feel different emotions and how might they feel?
- Think of times the student has felt angry, upset, anxious. How did it feel? Encourage them to draw it, write it or explain it.
- How could they recognise these feelings if they happen again?
- Reassurance that different feelings are experienced by everyone and we all have to find ways to manage them. Discuss and write down ways they could keep calm and what they could do if they recognise a physical sensation related to anger or anxiety.

Taking it Further

Students can make a booklet or 'Helping myself' sheet highlighting the emotion, how it feels to them and a strategy to use when they recognise it.

Traffic lights

'Help children to recognise when they are feeling unsettled and to learn how to help themselves feel better.'

If children can learn to recognise when they are calm, beginning to feel anxious or feeling out of control and are given a means of communicating this, then support can be put in place to prevent a spiralling of behaviour.

Often once this strategy is in place the student seldom uses it, but knowing the option is there helps in itself. Students need a way of letting you know they are struggling, whether with the level of work, the kind of activity or because they feel they need time to calm down. They need to let you or support staff know in an inconspicuous way that they need help.

The idea is that students have cards in the colours red, orange and green. These can be in the back of a diary that is kept on the desk. The card on top is green, but if the student is starting to find the task in hand difficult or if they have had a bad morning and the pupil next to them is unsettling them, they can move the card to orange. This indicates they need help: this could be further explanation, to be released from the task, or to be given quiet time. If the card is moved to red, this could signify that the student should not be questioned, or could mean they have not understood the task at all. The purpose and parameters of the cards will need to be discussed before implementation and will vary from child to child. Make sure they understand how and when the cards can be used. Write down the definitions to ensure there are no differences of opinion or confusion.

Barometer of emotion

'Help the student recognise emotions and respond appropriately.'

Students may need help noticing at what point their emotions change. They need support to recognise what calm, anxious or angry look and feel like for them. Once they begin to recognise these emotions in themselves, they can begin to regulate their emotions.

In the first instance, teaching about the different emotions is useful. To then explain how emotions can escalate from calmness to anxiety and/or to anger, the use of a worksheet showing a barometer or scale as a visual aid can be really useful. Encourage the student to recognise how they feel when they are calm, anxious and angry. You may need to talk them through this, for example: when calm their body may feel loose, cool and relaxed; when angry, fists may curl, their stomach may feel hot or their teeth clenched. Encourage them to use their own words to describe how it feels if they can. They may need to recall past times where they have felt angry. If it seems this is distressing the student, then stop.

Use the outline of a barometer, a speed dial, a vertical ladder or arc shaped scale. Mark the three emotions: calm, anxious, angry. If the student recognises phases in between then add another one or two emotions. The student may choose colours or draw faces to illustrate the emotion. Using Velcro or sticky tack, adhere an arrow to the scale. The student can then move the arrow to indicate how they are feeling. If they are moving the arrow slowly up the scale during a lesson, then they will need strategies in place to help them cope.

Teaching Tip

One student I know who works closely with a Teaching Assistant in mainstream uses this idea regularly. As he starts moving the arrow upwards, his TA will suggest calm breathing. If it continues to move upwards there are a number of strategies they work through including looking at special interest pictures and leaving the class for a short while. He then returns and moves the arrow back down. It works – give it a go.

Taking it Further

Customise the scale. If a student's special interest is cars, use a speedometer, if it is manga comics, use characters from manga to illustrate the emotions.

Feelings jar

'A lovely activity to help students recognise their feelings and help themselves.'

This idea is adapted from an activity outlined by Winston's Wish, a charity for supporting bereaved young people. This idea aims to help them remember loved ones they have lost by attributing colours to memories. I have adapted it for students with autism to help them identify and understand feelings and plan how to help themselves if distressed.

Teaching Tip

Place some cotton wool on top of the uppermost layer, then screw on the lid to compact the salt and preserve the layers.

Taking it Further

Share with parents. Students can take the jar home and the notes serve as a reminder. A copy could be kept in school.

Initially, you may need to discuss with the students a little about feelings, asking them: 'When you are at home on the computer, how do you feel?', 'When you got angry on Friday, how did you feel?'. Note four or five feelings down in a column. Next to that, encourage pupils to use words or drawings to describe how they feel, physically or emotionally. Finding images on the Internet that match how they feel may be easier for some. Ask them to decide on a colour they link to this emotion. In the last column, talk about what they could do to make them feel better if they are an angry red, for example, or how they could calm themselves if they are a nervous yellow.

The next stage is to make the feelings jar, to represent the fact that we are all made up of different emotions. The jar needs to be relatively small and have a screw top lid. Fill it with table salt, then tip the table salt out again into four or five equal piles, depending on how many emotions you have discussed. Place each pile on a sheet of A4 paper. Rub chalk pastels of the chosen colours into the salt to colour it. Once you have four or five different coloured piles of salt, carefully pour each one into the jar, one at a time, to create a layered effect.

Windows of opportunity

'When behaviour is repeatedly challenging, you may need to create space in the timetable to address the issue.'

Whilst all students should be included in lessons and encouraged to attend regularly, there may be times where additional behaviour support and help for the student with autism is required. It may be necessary to carve out some time in the school week where the student has extra support.

Initially it may be helpful to meet with the student and parents to discuss the behaviour and attempt to find any underlying cause. If all is reportedly fine at home then look to school issues. If there is something that can be done to support the student in the home, such as referrals to support services, leniency with homework or increased communication, then try that.

Many students with autism can struggle with forging friendships. This would be an initial area for exploration. Try to establish if the student is lonely, feeling bullied and how they spend their unstructured break times. It is likely there will be many students in the school who could benefit from some social skills support: perhaps for a half term, for an hour a week this could be prioritised. If they feel they have friendships and feel less likely to fail at socialising, they will be calmer in class.

Try to involve them during class sessions. If their behaviour is beginning to deteriorate, ask them to hand out the books, help you with your computer or find a means of distracting them. Use windows of time at the start or end of lesson or in tutorials to discuss, as a general topic, behaviour in class and how negative behaviour can impact on others.

Teaching Tip

If a student has a detention for poor behaviour, work with them on their behaviour management. Encourage them to write down concerns about or explanations for their behaviour.

Taking it Further

Make good use of break and lunch times. Guided social groups can be a great way of getting positive messages about behaviour and coping strategies over to the student.

School refusers

'Prevention is better than cure.'

Students with autism who run away from school, skip classes or do not attend are doing so for a reason. It is important to try to isolate causes for this as soon as possible. It can become very difficult to encourage them back into school when a pattern of absconding or refusal has been established.

Teaching Tip

A friend, sibling or responsible peer could be used as a buddy to support and help reintegrate the student back into school. They could be asked to sit with the student and perhaps meet them on arrival. The person would be familiar, and the aim is to make the reintegration as predictable and non anxiety-provoking as possible.

Taking it Further

Be creative and flexible with the timetable. If anxiety is high, create windows of time where the student can have calm time or time to talk through concerns with a member of staff. The start of the day is often a difficult time. If they are not coping with the level of work, then time and extra support may need to be given. The aim is to ensure the student attends. Once anxiety is reduced and he or she is coping, the usual timetable may be resumed.

If a student has suddenly begun to skip lessons or is refusing to attend, then something has changed in their lives or their thinking to cause them to stay away. It is important to work this out and get them back into school as soon as possible. The longer they are out of the system, the more of a struggle it will become for them to face returning. The difficulties with transition, anxiety and change will all make a return hugely challenging. Talk to the student and parents. Often, reassurance and simple changes can be made and the pupil will return to a typical attendance pattern. One student used to run home because, it transpired, he hated PE. Once he realised that it was quite nice being at home on that day, he began to run home more regularly. A lot of work with parents and the student had to then take place to get him back to school. Another student could not cope with unstructured time; she did not know how to fill it. She was offered the chance to go to the library during break and lunch times where she could read quietly.

Try to find out why the student does not want to attend. The following ideas may help:

- Talk with parents. They may need support with boundary setting. Many are exhausted and have tried everything. In some cases the student is far more challenging in the home than at school and parents need more help from external agencies.

- Talk with the student. If adjustments can be made to the curriculum, unstructured time or the journey to school then make these changes.
- If students have a more established pattern of non-attendance, then reintegrate slowly, choosing favoured subjects, ensuring they can keep on top of work. A modified curriculum may be necessary.
- Give them a named person and place to go if they are anxious. Someone could meet them on arrival.
- If students are absconding because of bullying, work or school reasons, then these need to be addressed and the student will need reassurance. If they are leaving because sitting at home on the Xbox is preferable, then work with parents on this being not permitted.
- When anxiety is so high that students cannot attend school, a longer term phased re-entry may need to be planned in detail. This may need to start with an initial visit, working in the library or a quiet room, gradually building up to an hour in mainstream class where the student goes early and knows where he or she is sitting in advance.

Intrusive talking

'I don't think he realises quite how much his continual talking disrupts the class.'

It may be that the student is repeatedly asking questions, they may be calling out, talking to their peers or echoing what has been said. Whatever the case, this kind of talk is intrusive and can make delivering a lesson and maintaining discipline difficult.

The student may not be aware he or she is calling out quite so much, or they may be echoing what is heard to help them process information, and repeated questioning may be a means of reassuring themselves. Persistent interruption of this kind, though, can be frustrating for teachers and pupils alike. Try the following:

- Ignore repetitive questions or, to give reassurance, give the answer by reframing what has been said to the whole class. If the question is 'what is the time?' then do not give a direct response but address the class saying 'right everyone, it is ten past twelve . . .'
- Set clear rules about speaking in class and display these rules so they are visible.
- Explain why the student's shouting out is a problem.
- Encourage students to note down questions or comments, or write them down on the whiteboard yourself for discussion at a later time.
- Praise periods of non-interruption.
- Remind the student discretely when they are echoing what you or others are saying or thinking out loud. They may not realise they are doing so.
- Use a card system to indicate when pupils are disrupting – this could be a whole-class strategy. You could use a yellow and red card warning, traffic lights, a barometer card to show when the disruption is getting too much, or a symbol of a person with fingers on lips.

Is it autism?

'Some children have more than one diagnosis and it can be difficult to know how to best support them.'

There are various syndromes and conditions that can present in similar ways. If you are unsure as to whether a student has autism or autism and another condition, you need to ensure this is sensitively communicated to relevant professionals and parents.

Generally, any developmental or ALN concerns are picked up at primary school but this is not always the case. You may feel that a student in your class is struggling with aspects of social, communication, processing or relationship development. Alternatively, you may just feel the student is not coping and that there may be an underlying reason. There are also times when you may feel that there is something else causing the student with autism difficulty and may suspect an additional condition is present. In such cases, it is important to discuss your concerns with the school ALNCo and with parents in a sensitive manner. It is likely that they will share your concerns and may have already considered seeking help but don't known where to start.

In some cases, parents may openly discuss their concerns and it may be appropriate to sensitively suggest they see their GP. If a diagnosis is progressed, then it is important that the family receive support in dealing with this. In the meantime, using the autism support strategies outlined in this book will be beneficial to all students and can do no harm. Simplifying language, making resources and instructions clear and using visual aids will help all pupils whether they have a diagnosis of autism and/or any other ALN.

Teaching Tip

If you have concerns about a student, it can be useful to keep notes about the behaviour shown, concerns around processing, understanding and learning and any other observations. These can be shared with parents and agencies if the need arises.

Taking it Further

If you are unable to discuss concerns with parents or they do not wish to pursue a diagnosis, then use of autism-friendly strategies will help. Information can be shared amongst staff and an IEP can be put in place to support areas of difficulty.

Social skills and relationship development

Part 5

Getting social interaction wrong

'It is like he is behind a sheet of glass, watching everyone interact. They look like him, sound like him, but he just can't break through. He keeps getting it wrong.'

Many young people with autism would say that forging and coping with the intricacies of social interaction is one of the most difficult aspects of the condition. At times, they are able to cope very well, learning about conversations and social communication. However, often, they can still get it wrong. Misunderstanding or not grasping social cues can leave them embarrassed or at a loss as to why they cannot maintain friendships.

Taking it Further

Drama classes or clubs can be a fantastic way of getting students feeling involved and socialising, and gives them the chance to explore their social selves in different roles. Liaise with the drama teacher and encourage autistic students to sign up to these clubs.

In class, the most important thing you can do is to be aware of this. The following ideas could help pupils improve social interaction in class and feel less daunted by it:

- Group work may be difficult for children with autism. Offer alternatives, or ensure the student is placed in an understanding, supportive group.
- Unstructured time can be lonely. Check that they have a place or a club to go to at lunch or break.
- If you know a student is struggling or lonely, support them by finding pupils with common interests. Some work may need to be done explaining what friendship is and what makes a good friend. A support assistant could be asked to do this. Some of the ideas that follow may also help.
- If you notice them 'getting it wrong', let them know. At a quiet time, go through what happened, why the other person responded as they did and importantly, what they should do next time to 'get it right'.
- If a topic lends itself, however tenuously, to teaching about social skills, make use of it.

Conversation maintenance

'He talks *at* me, not to me.'

You may notice that some students converse in a stilted or unusual way. They may not wait for responses, may go off on tangents or walk off half way through. They are not being rude, they're just struggling with understanding how a conversation works.

Many people with autism have written and spoken about how conversation and social interaction mystifies them. One student I taught would often instigate a conversation then walk away when she was no longer interested. When asked why, she said that if what the other person was saying was not interesting, then what was the point in staying?

Some students tend to talk in a monologue at the other person, perhaps about a special interest or concern. There is no reciprocity at all, no pausing whilst the other person responds. Other pupils may get the dialogue bit right but make mistakes owing to the use of non-literal language that appears in the conversation or because they misread or misuse facial expressions or gestures. You can help by:

- Reminding them that a conversation involves more than one person and that they need to listen and be heard.
- Help a pupil know the kind of questions that may appear in conversations and how they could respond.
- Make a mind map of the kind of topics they could discuss.
- Scripts of conversations and reminders to ask questions throughout a conversation can help, but make sure that the student doesn't stick so rigidly to what you tell them to say.
- Encourage them to practice conversing with people they trust.

Teaching Tip

Encourage the students to make a list of conversation starters and endings, so they can use them and recognise them as signals to the start and end of talking to another.

Bonus Idea ★

Show the students television clips of different types of conversation, and talk about what they notice. Soaps and some sitcoms are great for this.

Think it, pause, say it right

'This acts like a pause button, reminding the student to think before they speak.'

Some students with autism can appear rude because some of the things that they say can be hurtful or blunt. This idea can be used in and out of the classroom to encourage them to pause, filter or rethink what they want to say before saying it.

People with autism can struggle to interpret the thoughts and feelings of others. Situations that would ordinarily warrant a sympathetic or caring response may not be forthcoming from them. If, for example, a student fails a test badly, generally their peers would respond with consoling words or reassurance. The person with autism may respond by pointing out that the grade is a fail, whereas they got an A grade. This is not because the person is trying to be hurtful, but rather, they cannot observe any visible hurt nor can they perceive or 'mind read' emotions and feelings. They are just making an observation.

Give the student a flashcard with the words 'think', 'pause', 'speak', printed on it. People working with the student can then draw his or her attention to the card to help them notice when they are saying something inappropriate. The card could be stuck in a diary to serve as a reminder to: think about what they want to say, pause to think if it could be offensive, hurtful or inappropriate, and then say it in a polite way. Of course, some students will need help recognising what is appropriate or not and with speaking the truth politely.

Taking it Further

Discuss scenarios or watch video footage of inappropriate and appropriate verbal responses. Discuss different ways of making your point politely.

Bonus Idea ★

Think it, write it, say it right. The student could have cards on which they can write down their thoughts to help them process, consider what went wrong or ask another person for guidance.

Bullying vs. teasing

'She would complain of being bullied, but often the other children were just joking around. She struggles to tell the difference.'

Young people with autism may need help in recognising the difference between unkind, bullying behaviour and teasing or joking as a part of a game.

The first step is to ensure the student is not being bullied. If they are, then this needs to be dealt with (see Idea 58). If it is apparent that the student is confusing intentional mean behaviour with teasing then they will need support to:

- Help them recognise the difference between friendly teasing and unkindness.
- Respond appropriately to unfriendly teasing or bullying.
- Establish strategies of what to do when unsure.

Some ideas of how to address this include:

- Noting in columns what signifies bullying behaviour compared to harmless teasing. It is important to note the kind of words and actions that fit into these categories.
- Watching footage or clips of kind and unkind behaviour. What do the students notice about the body language, words used and facial expressions? How do we know this is kind or not?
- Use 'what would happen if?' scenario cards. Include more and less obvious instances of bullying. Have the student or group select a card and discuss how they know this is a form of bullying or not and what they would do about it.
- Make sure that the student knows what to do if they cannot workout the other person's behaviour, e.g. talk through the incident with a peer or teacher.

> **Bonus Idea** ★
>
> Get a group of students with and without autism together. Write some scenarios involving bullying or friendly teasing on flash cards. Encourage students to problem-solve the scenarios together.

Non-verbal cues

'Facial expressions and body language – those unspoken human nuances – can completely change the meaning of what is said.'

Facial expressions, body language and gesture accompany spoken language, adding meaning and emotion. People with autism can miss these non-verbal cues and so misinterpret what is being said or inferred. They need help in learning how to use and recognise this part of social interaction.

People working with children with autism need to be aware that these individuals may struggle to interpret the non-verbal intricacies of social interaction. This can have a massive impact on their ability to forge and sustain relationships and cause much confusion. A raised eyebrow, widening of the eyes or biting of the lip can indicate uncertainty, disbelief or concern, depending on the context of what is being said. Young people with autism can completely miss these cues. A peer may say, 'Simon was so helpful.' The student with autism will have no reason to take this other than literally and will 'file away' that information. The fact that the comment about Simon was said with raised eyebrows and a slight shake of the head gives it a whole different meaning, which may have not been perceived by the person with autism. Often, sarcasm, jokes and exaggerated stories are spoken with subtle changes to voice, body language or facial expression that completely change the meaning of what is said.

Students with autism need help learning how to recognise these subtle non-verbal cues. Try out some of the following ideas:

• There are some good websites and programmes that can be purchased which help with teaching non-verbal social cues. There are also many YouTube videos that teach this; watch them carefully in advance to make sure they are appropriate, but they can be very helpful.

- Make your own facial expression booklet. Encourage the student to look online or through magazines and identify, print and cut out as many different examples as they can of different facial expressions. Create pages for different emotions: happy, sad, sarcastic, surprised. Some are difficult to tell apart from one another.

- Watch comedy shows or dramas and encourage the students to identify sarcasm or inference. Some video clips on YouTube or other sites have isolated clips perfect for this kind of analysis.

- Get them to act out a short interaction with and then without facial expression or gesture. How does facial expression and body language change the meaning? If possible, video the interactions and watch them back with the students.

- Encourage students to try to recognise non-verbal cues as they arise in everyday interaction.

Managing the bully and the bullied

'If a student with autism is bullied, then they and the bully will need to be managed carefully.'

Students with autism may not always realise they are being bullied. They may play the joker, thinking they are 'fitting in' when actually they are being laughed at. It is a delicate issue as the student with autism will not want to be singled out, but any bullying must be dealt with as soon as it arises.

Teaching Tip

A whole-school approach towards bullying will ensure consistent approaches to tackling it. Encourage other students to 'speak up' if they feel one of their peers is being bullied.

Taking it Further

If the strategies in this idea do not work then often the threat of a school carrying out of a meeting with the parents of the bully will make them think twice, but this does of course presuppose that the parents are supportive or available to meet, which may not always be the case.

Depending on the nature of the bullying, sanctions will need to be used to deter future incidents. It can help to get the person who has been unkind to sit down with the person with autism. Often when they hear the impact that their behaviour has had, they will see the error of their ways. The person with autism may need help expressing how they feel. It may be necessary for you to explain.

If the student and parents are open about the diagnosis and feel that discussing this could help, then it can be very useful to explain about autism to the person or people doing the bullying. One boy was often taunted by his peers but he went along with it. He knew it was not right but at least, as he saw it, he had friends. Some work was carried out with him about friendships. The bullies were encouraged to support and look out for him rather than ridicule him and some information about the condition was shared with them. They embraced the idea of being his protector and the boy was included in the group. This will not work in all cases and any peer discussion about a student's condition needs to be done with consent and with caution.

Teach, practice, repeat

'These skills will need to be taught time and time again and in different contexts for some students with autism.'

The teaching of social and communication skills is necessary for most students with autism. Once they have learned some of the 'rules' of social interaction, they then have to adapt them to a range of different social situations, environments and people. This requires repeated practice.

Some of the main social skills that those with autism may need support with are:

- Conversation skills: avoiding monologue, conversation safe topics, starters and ends. Recognising when another person is trying to start or end a conversation.
- Understanding what tone of voice and way of talking to use when and with whom, for example, the way they would speak to their friends will differ from conversations with the headteacher.
- Learning what is polite and impolite to say.
- Being aware of the personal space of others.
- Recognising facial expression, gesture and body language.

Some students excel at teaching themselves how to recognise facial expressions and how to use them themselves. Others will need a lot of help in learning and generalising the skill. The more often it is taught and in different situations the better. Practice these skills through:

- Role play. Videoing and watching this back is very useful.
- Conversation and facial expression cards. Cards with scripts of conversation, pictures or thought bubbles on. What is the person trying to do or say and how do we know?
- One-to-one teaching may be required before moving on to group work.

Taking it Further

These skills can be practised in the community – in shops, libraries, cafés or when buying tickets for public transport. School trips and social skills outings also provide opportunities for social interaction, and parents can get involved too by encouraging their child to interact in different environments.

Buddying up

'He learned more in the time spent with his peer mentor about social interaction than I could ever teach him.'

Students with autism often want to fit in and make friends. In most cases, teaching them about social skills is not enough. The pupils need to put skills into practice. Spending time with a carefully chosen buddy can help them learn more and try out these skills.

Spending time with a peer mentor or 'buddy' provides the student with the opportunity to practise their social skills in a wider range of places and do more activities than they can do alone. Students with autism tend to be visual learners and will be able to observe and echo some of the skills they see their buddy use. Of course, the choice of a buddy needs to be carefully made and they need to be prepared to commit. Some sixth form pupils are happy to take on this mentor role but responsible pupils from their own year group would be ideal.

It may be that the buddy is needed for certain times such as break times or on the bus to school. Alternatively, time could be scheduled on the weekly timetable to work with the student. Ideally, they will have spent some social time with one another. A colleague of mine once arranged weekly meetings in a chosen room, where the peer mentors and selected students met, played games and got to know each other. Over time they met in and out of school depending on the needs and wishes of the student with autism. This idea does involve a little work, ensuring a room is found and regular slots are timetabled, but in the long run it will reduce problems and increase students' confidence.

Bonus Idea ★

Put cards in a box to promote discussions between the buddy and student with autism – they can pick one or two cards out to discuss in each session. The topic on the cards could help them get to know one another or work through scenarios that they could then put into practice in day-to-day life.

Turn taking and waiting

'Waiting around is unstructured time. Some students with autism struggle to cope with this.'

There are countless situations, in and out of school, when pupils are expected to wait patiently. Students with autism can find this period of waiting difficult to manage as there is nothing to do, no guidance and no set timeframe. They need help coping with this and with their responses to others involved.

Students with autism often find waiting for something difficult. They may struggle to see why they should wait their turn in a queue, for example, when they need to get to the front now. The rigidity of their thinking or the intense draw of a special interest may mean that they pay no heed to social waiting norms.

To teach the skill of waiting, try the following:

- Have a card on which they can write down what they want to say. They may become frustrated and worry that if they are not permitted to speak they will forget what they wanted to say.
- Where possible, give them an activity to do during unstructured time.
- Practice waiting with different people and in different situations.
- If waiting for a turn during a game or before doing an activity in class, visual cues could help. Use cards: red to indicate 'wait' and green for 'go'. Put pupils in alphabetical or some other order, so the pupil can see a logic and structure to the waiting.
- Use of comic strip conversations or 'social stories' can help the pupil understand the reason for waiting (see Idea 33).

Teaching Tip

In your lessons, keep a clock or timer visible and indicate clearly how long the student will have to wait between tasks.

Social support book

'These booklets are individualised to suit the student and their needs.'

This resource is made up of pages that reassure the students, by teaching new skills and consolidating past teaching. It can be adapted and added to. It should be discreet and of a size that can be carried easily in their school bags.

Teaching Tip

Make the booklet visual. The student can personalise the file to make it appealing. Also use visual mind maps and pictures to help develop ideas.

A social support booklet includes pages that remind the student how to cope with social interaction. Divide it into sections such as: conversation, language, scenarios and keeping calm.

- Conversation: Sample starters and endings. A list of topics that are good to discuss and those to avoid. Top tips about avoiding monologue, listening and asking questions.
- Language: A list of idioms and their meanings, what to do if you have not understood, how to recognise sarcasm. A table showing friendly and unfriendly language and behaviour.
- Scenarios: What would I do if . . .? With solutions and 'social stories' to help the pupil out of certain situations.
- Keeping calm: A list of things that can calm them, the name and photo of the person and place to go when anxious, a timetable, special interest cards, time out cards.

You could also include a pen portrait or Person Centred Plan in the booklet so that if the student gets distressed they can show it to the teacher.

These are just some ideas. The student can add whatever they feel helps them to their social support booklet.

Hello, goodbye and in-between

'If the student can cope with conversations, they will be better able to forge and sustain friendships.'

People with autism can struggle to make conversation. Often, it is difficult for them to remember all of the social 'rules', so giving them tools to help them start and end conversations and teaching them ways of coping if they do not understand can really help.

One student explained that just thinking about starting a conversation would panic her. She didn't know how to start and worried if she did, she may not cope with further interaction or might say something inappropriate. She could not bring herself to even try talking to her peers in case she got it wrong.

The following ideas will help the student feel more confident beginning and ending conversations, and will help them to cope if it all gets a bit confusing.

- Discuss appropriate ways of greeting and saying goodbye to people. Make a spider diagram of conversation starters and endings.
- Role-play examples or watch a film or TV programme. Discuss what worked and what didn't.
- When watching video footage, encourage the students to notice any gestures that people make. If eye contact is hard for the pupil then a wave or a thumbs-up to signal they want to join in can work.
- If the student cannot understand what has been said, did not have time to process it or lost interest, give them some ideas of what they could say: 'Sorry, I didn't hear what you said' or 'Can you say that again? I got distracted.'
- Discuss scenarios for if they want to leave the conversation.

Teaching Tip

Make some small laminated cards for the student to keep with conversation starters on one side and endings on the other.

Taking it Further

The pupil may also need help recognising signs such as yawning, not participating or looking away which often indicate the other person is disinterested.

Peer support

'Help the peer group understand the condition.'

If we can help young people understand more about autism and what it means for the people who have a diagnosis, then they will be more friendly and supportive peers. We can all be wary of what we do not understand so it is important to encourage a whole-school level of awareness and understanding.

In enhancing peer understanding of autism across the year groups you will be helping to foster a positive, whole-school attitude towards those with the condition. It will aid inclusion and help those with autism feel more accepted and confident in school. Often, in the first week of transition into Year 7, there is some time when class or group activities are carried out. This would be an ideal time to do some work around autism. If it is tackled in Year 7, then as the pupils move through school, the positive ethos should move with them and have a ripple effect across age groups. Alternatively, a few sessions could be embedded into the PSHE curriculum.

You could create and use a booklet to encourage thinking about autism. Many students with autism are glad to have their condition understood, but it needs to be managed carefully. Ensure that whilst the areas of difficulty are explained, they are done so with examples so students can put it into context. Make sure the strengths of those with autism are also discussed: their focus, honesty, ability to retain information and their knowledge of their special interests. Get the class thinking about what they could say and do to be friendly and supportive towards those with autism in school.

Student posters

'Visual displays or posters that catch your eye are a great way to teach about autism.'

The use of posters and displays around the school is a great way of helping everyone to gain a greater understanding of autism. If you can get the children involved in researching and creating these displays together then this will enhance the learning experience.

Create displays celebrating the success of people with autism such as artists or poets, and articles about or written by people with autism. Information about the condition could be clearly displayed alongside support methods. The general feeling or message that needs to underpin this work is one of acceptance and support.

Get all students involved in researching the condition and designing and creating their own posters. This activity could slot in with the work on raising peer awareness or as a part of another mainstream curricular subject. In getting the class involved there is a stronger likelihood that the message will stick with them and spread more widely. As other students see these posters popping up around school, the message embeds further.

Encourage pupils to adopt autism friendly strategies in their posters such as clear writing, simple and direct language, use of colour to highlight key facts and drawings to illustrate and add clarity. Encourage students to develop information leaflets or projects to deliver to the class or share in assemblies for more in-depth work.

Taking it Further

Encourage students to create PowerPoint displays or talks to share with your class or a wider audience as a part of an autism awareness day or week.

Life skills

'We need to teach life skills to help the student become more independent out of school.'

Seize any opportunity to work with young people with autism on life skills. All pupils will benefit, but the student with autism may really need support with many of the life skills we take for granted. Just because they are exceptional at maths, this doesn't mean they will be able to cope with handling money in a supermarket.

It is important to remember that students with autism cannot always transfer skills. In the school environment, there is a reasonable amount of structure. Many pupils bring their own packed lunch and mix with a restricted group of people. In the wider community, a different set of skills is required. They need to learn to handle money, wait for change, order their food, catch public transport and cope when they get things wrong. We may feel that the student has learned social and communication skills in school, they may even be using them well with staff and peers, however, remembering to use what they have learned outside of school can be difficult for some.

Role-playing activities can be a great start, but the skills then need to be rehearsed in real life. A good way to start promoting independence skills is to encourage the pupils to carry out tasks in the school environment first, e.g. by taking out a book from the library or by ordering and paying for dinner in the canteen if they usually have packed lunch. School trips and visits provide great opportunities for trying out life skills. Staff should use this time to monitor, guide and teach road safety, the process of purchasing goods and finding their way around a place. Encourage pupils to use the school canteen and library if they are not already doing so. They may need support initially, but should be encouraged to move towards independence.

Where possible teach life skills across the curriculum. As relevant topics arise, plan practical sessions where students can rehearse the different skills. For example, reading timetables, handling money and saving money could all be taught through maths lessons; writing a CV, communicating through writing and information-seeking can be taught in English lessons; and pricing up ingredients, preparing and cooking healthy meals can be taught through food technology. Encourage parents to support their child's life skills by helping them form a personal care routine and by involving their child in household tasks such as doing the laundry, in order to enhance their application of these skills.

The physical environment and sensory considerations

Part 6

Classroom environment

'One student would flatly refuse to go to a certain classroom because he said it felt wrong. This was not helped by a class layout that changed frequently, and with chewing gum and graffiti on the desks.'

Students with autism will be more likely to stay on task and are less likely to be disruptive if they feel safe in their classroom and know what is expected of them in this environment. Minimise change and potential distractions and the student will be able to focus on the set work rather than trying to feel calm and in control.

Teaching Tip

If nothing else, de-clutter the classroom, removing litter and graffiti, unnecessary and distracting posters, old notices or piles of paperwork.

The look, layout and sensory aspects of a room can determine how we feel. A stuffy room with dirty desks and chairs scraping on tiled floors could well distract from learning. Equally, a classroom that has a different layout or seating plan every half term could leave students with autism feeling confused and uncomfortable. Ideally, keep classrooms clutter free, desks clean, seating plans consistent and distractions to a minumum. The following can help students with autism feel more at ease:

- Keep class rules consistent.
- Resist changing the class layout too frequently and give advance notice where possible.
- Keep things in their designated place.
- Minimise distractions.
- Ensure a clear view of any whiteboards or visual aids.
- Avoid sitting the students in groups if this distracts them.
- Ensure the room is light and airy.
- Be aware of sensory considerations in the room.
- Students with autism can benefit from having a consistent seat in clear sight of the board and near the front of the class.

Bonus Idea ★

Carry out a sensory audit of the classroom. The Autism Education Trust have a straightforward, detailed template: tinyurl.com/jalj36l.

Everything in its right place

'There is less excuse for roaming around the class looking for things. It definitely feels calmer.'

This idea makes the classroom look tidier, the environment feel calmer and saves time. The result is a greater sense of order and predictability that will appeal to and greatly help young people with autism. Time is saved and behaviour improves, because everyone knows where everything is kept. There is no unstructured hunting for paper or tripping over coats.

This idea can take time to implement but is well worthwhile. Keeping an ordered, tidy environment may seem insignificant, but it seems to inspire a sense of order and control in the people within it! All students will benefit from this, but those with autism will have an environment that is more predictable and so feels more safe to them. Firstly, you need to ensure that the classroom is decluttered and is generally tidy. Then implement the following:

- Allocate a place for students to store coats and bags.
- Find a place for homework or completed work to be collected in and stored.
- Chairs behind tables, litter in bins and nothing blocking walk ways at the end of each lesson.
- Store spare equipment, stationery or textbooks where easily accessible.
- Keep spare paper, resources and textbooks in clearly labelled boxes – everything to go to where it came from.
- Store any potentially messy resources such as paint out of reach.
- Make sure notices are displayed in the same place, ideally on a notice board that students know to check.

Visual reminders

'Visual reminders, instructions and timetables allow the student to process all of the relevant information in their own time.'

Having information presented visually can be useful for students with autism. If they are unable to process what is being said or tend to forget what has been asked of them, then visual reminders ease pressure and help them to cope during the busy school day.

The use of visual cues and reminders in the classroom environment can help students with autism feel more in control and ensures they do not miss out on information. This could take the form of a notice board in the tutor group, with class timetables and any changes to routine shown on it. Calendars can be used to show an overview of events with important dates such as exam dates highlighted.

If there are several tasks to complete or multiple instructions then list them clearly for students to follow. Display class rules or behaviour support systems so that you and the students can refer to them.

Less able pupils may benefit from more visual timetables, with colour coding or pictures to indicate the different subjects clearly. Give them a laminated version with a sticker on it that they can move along the squares as the day and lessons progress.

On the board or on a pupil sheet, write two headings in two columns: 'Now' and 'Next'. Under each heading, write what the topic of the lesson will be and where the class are going to next, e.g.: 'Now: Technology – Revising our designs'. 'Next: Maths, room 112, Mr Brown'.

Potential playground problems

'I hate break times. There is nothing to do and the playground is noisy, dirty and stressful.'

In classrooms there will be some structure and routine in a relatively small and familiar space. The playground is often a large, intimidating and unpredictable environment. Some students will find it difficult to cope with unstructured time in such a place.

Every person with autism will have their own idea about how they wish to spend their break and lunch times. Some will need that time to just walk, be alone and have time to calm down and process a busy morning or afternoon of work and socialising. If this is their preference, the student should be allowed time to do so. One pupil I taught was very calm in lesson times but at break times would walk round and round the perimeter of the playground flapping. This appeared to serve as a release of tension and enabled a calm return to class.

Others will find unstructured time difficult to manage. It may be necessary to agree on a designated place for the student to go: the library, a withdrawal room or a bench where they can read or play games on their phone. The student may prefer to stay indoors with a friend, or a buddy system could be used. Ideally, lunchtime clubs would be available as another option for some days of the week.

Teaching Tip

Have a named place and person for the student to go to if they cannot cope or feel bullied or lonely. Talk with them to determine a place and/ or person that they can go to at times of distress. The location needs to be safe, with people nearby but perhaps not too crowded, and the person would need to be always available. It may therefore be useful to have two named people in case one is absent.

Halls, canteens and specialist classrooms

'Every time she sat in assembly she would fidget, move her chair and distract others. She could not be still and just listen.'

Certain environments can be more stressful than others owing to the size, acoustics and activities that happen within them. There are some strategies that can be used to make these environments more manageable for the person with autism. There may be occasions, however, where you will need to consider whether or not they take part in an activity in a certain space if it distresses them.

Teaching Tip

Similar issues can arise in canteens and larger, less structured classrooms such as in technology, art or the science labs. These can all have greater sensory challenges, requiring the students to follow slightly different rules and be a little less predictable. If students can have designated seats in these environments, have a Time out or Calm time card to enable them to leave if it gets too much, this may help.

Taking it Further

Allow students an early lunch pass, which allows them to leave the lesson a couple of minutes early so they can get their lunch and take it to a quiet place to eat it before the lunch time rush.

The school hall, and the assemblies or concerts held in this environment, can be stressful for students with autism. The room itself is often an open, echoing space with various sensory distractions. In addition, students are often expected to sit for lengths of time listening and watching in silence. This can be very difficult for the student with autism who struggles with unstructured time and may find the act of sitting still for 20 minutes or more, listening to unclear, echoing speeches, a painful experience. To feel more at ease, grounded and in control of time and space, the student may rock, fidget or pay no attention to what is being said as they are too distracted by sensory concerns. Therefore, events in the school hall may not be possible for some pupils and they may need to spend the time doing other tasks, instead being provided with a handout of any useful information they may have missed in assembly. Some students may be able to access part of the assembly or concert but may need to sit on the edge of the row, near the back so that they can leave if necessary. They could be permitted to take a lump of sticky tac, or a sensory toy into the room to help calm and distract them.

Changing rooms

'Some students will cope with new environments well but struggle when changes are made to familiar settings.'

There will be times that the teaching room changes or another setting is required for a certain lesson. The student with autism will need preparation for this.

If the lesson is due to take place in a different room for a period of time or just for a single session, give the student advanced warning. Hopefully they will be familiar with the new setting but if not, it is worth showing them the room in advance. Consider any sensory issues that may impact the student. If they struggle with these kind of changes then they could be allowed to choose a place to sit in advance and be informed of what the lesson will entail. This removes a little of the unpredictability for the pupil.

If the usual teaching classroom is changing, do forewarn the pupils. Be aware that changes to paint colour, lighting, carpet or fabrics will change the sense of space. The smell of new paint could be overwhelming and if carpets are removed then acoustics will be different. If the student walks into class to be confronted with a new class layout with a different sensory experience, this can be overwhelming. A student I taught became very unsettled when his English classroom was redecorated. He explained that he had found the change unsettling because it 'felt different'. The class layout had also been changed slightly. Although in the same position, his desk had been moved closer to the window, which he found distracting.

Teaching Tip

A change to the classroom could make an autistic student anxious. Keep other routines and structure the same, and allow the student to see the room at a quiet time, in advance, and to choose a seat. Minimising other changes will help the him or her cope with the change in class.

91

Be sensitive

'The sensory environment is very important for autistic people. They lack the ability to adjust to sensory assaults other people accept as normal.' (Bogdashina, 2003)

It is not always clear if or in what ways a person is struggling with sensory difficulties. Try to establish if a student is struggling with sensory issues by noting their behaviour and responses in different environments. Try to 'sense' the world from their perspective.

Teaching Tip

Flapping, tapping or rocking can indicate that the student is stressed and is trying to calm and regulate themselves. These repetitive types of behaviours can be calming and help give a sense of control so teachers need to take care before asking them to stop this.

The first step is taking the time to think through any behaviour or responses to certain tasks or settings and consider if it could be a result of too much or too little sensory input.

A student may be hyper-sensory and struggling to cope with too much sensory information if they make repetitive movements or noises to drown out other more frightening sensory experiences. They may appear jumpy or frightened of certain noises, shield themselves from light, dislike wearing certain fabrics or touching certain texture in food or materials such as paint or washing-up liquid. The sound of the hand dryer in the toilets or the smell of the canteen may be overwhelming for these children. They will avoid these experiences if possible or could become angry, distressed and lack focus as they try to filter some of this sensory invasion.

A student who appears to drift off, staring at certain colours, the branches moving on a tree or flickering lights may be hypo-sensory or lacking sensory stimulation. They may also try to gain sensory input by creating or gravitating towards noise, seeking pressure and appearing to enjoy strong smells and rocking or swinging. These children may appear intensely preoccupied with things and so are not paying attention in class. They could swing on their chair and be unable to resist tapping the desk.

Taking it Further

Make a list of behaviours the student exhibits. Do these fit with a hyper or hypo-sensory profile? Olga Bogdashina's book, see References p127, has an excellent sensory profile checklist.

Autism-friendly space

'Setting up an area or base for pupils with autism reassures the students and helps the staff.'

If a pupil with autism is stressed, anxious or feels that they need calm time, then they will benefit greatly from having a specific place that they can go to as and when needed. You can be creative with how you establish this to meet individual students' needs.

It is important that the pupil has a specific place that they feel happy going to when unsettled or unhappy. This can be written into an IEP or behaviour support plan. If necessary, resources or strategies such as time out cards will need to be used so the student knows that staff will permit them to leave class or their desk and access the space as needed.

The space could be a designated corner of the classroom that is set up as a quiet working area, a computer desk in the library or a specialist staffed base. Whatever is agreed between staff, students and parents, the space will need to be calm, with limited distractions and where staff are not too far away. A set of activities such as reading, drawing or playing suitable games on the computer could be agreed and the materials kept in the space or nearby. The aim of the space is to calm, reassure and de-escalate any unsettled behaviour.

It is important to make clear to the student that this space is to be used only when needed. Equally, staff need to be aware that if the student is very unsettled and requesting to use the space, some kind of supervision will be required. Clear communication between staff will be essential in such cases.

Teaching Tip

At break and lunch times, it can help if the student has a certain place that they can go to sit to relax. Again, this could be a desk in the classroom or a bench in the playground.

Bonus Idea ★

It can be useful to have a plan B. Give the student an alternative option if their usual space is not usable.

Sensible support

'If you can just try to imagine what sensory issues could be causing problems, you can then start trying to find solutions.'

There are some very simple ideas that can support students who are experiencing sensory difficulties. Once you have considered the behaviours or responses that the child is showing and established that they may need a reduction or increase in stimulation, you can consider how this can be addressed and supported during the school day.

Teaching Tip

Remember, if you have changed the class layout or seating plans this could have sensory implications for the student. If they are very sensitive to certain sensory stimuli, it may help to give them a card that explains this and permits them to leave if, for example, the noise of building work in an adjacent room or the smell of burning in a cookery class is too overwhelming.

If you think a student's challenging behaviour is a result of their sensory concerns, the most important thing to do in the first instance is not to react. If a student is refusing to take their hood down or stop tapping the desk, it is important to think why they are doing so. If you can address the underlying cause, then the behaviours may not manifest. The following ideas will not work in all settings or lessons but are worth consideration:

- Is the lightning flickering or buzzing? Are chairs scraping on floors, draughts blowing through windows or computer screens flickering? Try to sit the student away from these areas and get the problems resolved.
- Could the student wear ear defenders or listen to music? This will not always be acceptable, but during independent tasks or in a noisy technology room where machinery may be troubling, this could be permitted.
- In noisy rooms the student may not be able to pick out the teacher's words from the many other voices or noises. Filtering and processing information can then be very difficult. If a student appears to be drifting off or unable to focus owing to sensory overload, try the sticky tac approach, and check they have understood what you're saying and repeat if necessary.

- Some students have said that carrying their bag with them at all times helps calm them, giving sensory input and 'grounding' them.
- Some may benefit from special cushions or seating. The slight movement these affords can help regulate them.
- Some students will struggle to sit still for any length of time and may require movement breaks. Teachers can support this by asking the pupil to help by giving out books, collecting in work or handing out equipment.
- A quiet corner of the room or seating facing a wall and away from distractions may help the pupil focus on work.
- Leaving class a minute or two early, to avoid corridor crushes can help some students.
- Sensory overload in canteens and sports halls could mean students need to be allowed time out of these environments. Break and lunch times can pose different sensory challenges for pupils. Noisy canteens or busy playgrounds can be overwhelming. The student may need alternative places to go.

Bonus Idea

The student could keep with them a folder or small box of things that can help to regulate them as needed. This could include a swatch of material, sticky tack, a 'get out of class early' card to avoid the rush, and anything that calms them and supports their sensory needs. This folder can accompany them on the school bus, at home and at school.

Setting up a specialist base

'An autism base can be helpful for students with autism who struggle to cope with a full mainstream timetable or need more structure to their day.'

Students can go to the base knowing that their needs are understood and supported there. It should be a place of calm and structure where the pupil can go if unsettled or in need of additional social, communication or life skills lessons.

The establishment of a specialist base can be helpful in an environment where there are many students with autism who require additional support. How the room is established will depend on space and resource restrictions. Ideally the base should be staffed all day, including break and lunch times. If this is not possible, staff it for specific parts of the day e.g. first thing in the morning, the end of the day and for social skills groups. Transition times, at the start and the end of the day, can be a struggle for some pupils, so having a base where they can spend the unstructured time before registration or first lesson can be useful.

The base should be calm with minimal distractions and clutter. Displays should be simple and could endorse social or communication skills. Ideally, the room could have workstations or designated bays where students can work without distraction. A corner with beanbags can be useful to encourage social time or to act as a calming space. Use a noticeboard to display changes to routine, class rules and copies of timetables.

A specialist base, with staff who have had some training in autism and associated needs, can also be hugely reassuring for parents of anxious, unsettled children or those requiring more learning support.

Curriculum, testing and homework

Part 7

Simplify

'It's just too much.'

Whether writing on the board, sharing information from the web on a whiteboard or providing textbooks and worksheets, the way information is presented can have a massive impact on how the learner is able to process what is on the page or screen.

If you want a student with autism to get the most from a lesson then it is essential that it is presented to them clearly. This starts by the class teacher explaining the task with unambiguous language and perhaps writing the main pointers down on the board. Often tasks set involving textbooks or worksheets can be problematic for students with autism because of the amount of text on them, and pupils can feel overwhelmed before they even begin. To help avoid wasting time, causing stress and to ensure greater output of work:

- Make sure text is clear. If photocopied, ensure it is not blurred or words are not cut off.
- Avoid cursive script and make the writing a larger font or increase the size on the photocopier.
- A double page full of text is daunting and demoralising. Choose texts that are laid out clearly and are easy to read, ideally with diagrams.
- Some students will find a page full of black and white text difficult to read. Different coloured font can help prevent the text 'swimming' and blurring.
- You may need to reduce the amount of text. Some students will not be able to infer or pick out the relevant information from a sea of text. A busy layout can prevent them processing and selecting relevant sections of writing.

Using special interests

'It was impossible to get him to focus on writing a newspaper article on sport, so we agreed he could write about trains and I have never seen him work so hard.'

If a student with autism is struggling to grasp a concept, focus on a task or complete work, then involving their special interest or hobby can be a surprisingly effective way at getting them engaged. This can be used creatively across most subjects from time to time.

There is no escaping certain assessed or set tasks that must be delivered in a certain way. Generally there are opportunities to slightly alter the task or the way it is taught to better engage students and encourage higher quality and quantity of work. Try the following ideas:

- In written tasks such as story writing, allow the student to involve their special interest.
- The student's special interest or hobby could form a part of any work involving use of the library or researching information texts.
- Use pictures of the special interest on worksheets, IEPs or workbooks to engage students.
- Implement 'special interest time' as a reward or incentive, or use it as calming time.
- In topic work or artwork, make links to the special interest, allowing the student to incorporate it into their work or allowing further study into it after the set work is complete.
- Use the special interest to help focus attention. One student who could not focus for long enough to grasp a mathematical concept managed surprisingly well when it was taught using his special interest of cars.

Teaching Tip

Pupils with autism will often have impressive amounts of knowledge about their special interest. Allowing them to share it in class in some way can really help to boost their self-esteem.

Bonus Idea ★

Create a bank of special interest themed resources to support students with autism. This could include writing frames, talk time cards or reward sheets. Having them to hand will save time.

Differentiation

'Differentiating makes all the difference.'

Differentiating for students with autism in the classroom need not be time consuming and many of these resources, once created, can be used time and again and for different tasks and subjects.

Taking it Further

If a student can't cope with whole class presentations, reduce the group size, have them present to just their teacher one-on-one, or record their presentation and play the video back. Support pupils in advance of the lesson by giving notice of topics and lists of topic-related vocabulary. This will aid processing.

If we acknowledge that pupils with autism are likely to have difficulties with social understanding, communication and flexibility of thinking, then it follows that they may need support or a slightly different approach to teaching and learning. TAs can help by ensuring understanding and prompting and supporting tasks, but you also have to ensure that individuals with autism in your classroom have the work differentiated and delivered in a suitable way.

- Provide written instructions, task lists, vocabulary and step-by-step guides.
- If there are multiple tasks or activities, encourage pupils to cross off the tasks as they are achieved so that they can keep track of where they are.
- Use visual supports such as diagrams, posters, pictures and books to get meaning across.
- If pupils struggle with attention control, using a timer or clock can help them feel in control by knowing how long they need to work on a given task.
- Use iPads, video clips and interactive games to aid learning.
- If output is low or slow, provide cloze procedure activities, partly completed diagrams or cut and paste activities. All of these require the student to do the same work but take the pressure off by reducing large amounts of writing or drawing.

- Pupils could use a highlighter pen to identify key points in a text or to show they are able to find the answers.
- Questions may need to be rephrased. Inference can be difficult for pupils with autism. Questions on feeling and emotion may be problematic.
- Make sure supporting resources such as word books, dictionaries, times tables squares or number lines are to hand if needed.
- Whatever the subject, simplify any worksheets or information sheets to make them easily readable. Avoid using resources with lots of dense, small-font text.
- Use mind maps, tables, Venn diagrams and other alternative means of recording information.
- Writing frames, story starters, pictures and prompts can help with creative story writing.
- If the student is struggling to grasp a topic by traditional methods, use games, the Internet or computer activities. You could also use their special interests to sustain their attention.
- Provide alternative ways of completing activities where necessary. Pupils may not cope with the smell of the Bunsen burner, the texture of paint or the physical contact of rugby, for instance – so use the Internet to watch experiments, use different media for art and try smaller group work for some of the PE sessions.

ASC

'Before teaching or as problems arise, ask yourself, have you considered these three points?'

When teaching students with autism, bear in mind the following areas prior to teaching. The student will be more likely to achieve the learning outcomes of the lesson and less likely to display challenging behaviour if these three points are implemented.

Teaching Tip

If the student is still struggling to cope and the ASC points do not help you understand why, then consider potential sensory issues.

Adjustment. Students with ALN have a condition that can impact the way they learn and the amount they can process. We have to make reasonable adjustments to ensure that they are not at a disadvantage. Adjustment may be in the form of differentiating work, altering your expectations of the quality or output of their work, or changing how a lesson is delivered. You may also have to adjust how you manage support, sanction and praise.

Social implications. Check that the demands you are placing on the students are not too high. If you expect them to engage in group work, deliver presentations or join in with team games you may be asking too much. Consider whether the tasks presume an emotional understanding that may be difficult for them.

Communication. Theirs and yours! Has the lesson been delivered in a way that the student can comprehend? Are visual aids, worksheets and resources unambiguous and easy to understand? Is your language clear and literal and are instructions understood and reiterated if necessary? If the student struggles to communicate or communicates through challenging behaviour, in what ways can you enable them to express themselves? One-to-one time may need to be prioritised to ensure learning and understanding are achieved.

Supply teaching

'Supply teachers need to be aware of the students with ALN in their class and how best to support them.'

All teachers will have slightly different teaching styles and ways of delivering the curriculum. Changes to teaching and support staff can be disconcerting for some students. Consistency in approach and information sharing helps lessons run more smoothly.

Supply teachers or new support staff are a form of change and, as noted in the previous section on transition, change is difficult for many pupils with autism. If possible the student should be told in advance of such changes and whether they are long or short term. Some will cope fine with short-term change and if the teacher will be covering for the longer term, then the student will need to adapt. However, some students will struggle with a new teacher. The manner of delivery, tone of voice, the way they manage classroom discipline and expectations of the class may differ markedly from the usual teacher. At times, for the odd lesson, the student may need to have the work given to them to complete in an alternative classroom or the library if they cannot cope.

Supply teachers and support staff should be aware of the pupil with autism in their class, know the best way to support them and how to manage if behaviour becomes challenging. If the usual teacher gives the student an overview of the lesson in advance or writes the tasks on the board then the supply teacher should follow suit. Ideally, key information about the student will be handed to the supply staff to ensure change is minimised. This could be through a person centred plan or a note on the internal electronic register.

Teaching Tip

If information about the students with autism is not available but there is a support assistant in the class, ask them to explain to the supply teacher any support or strategies that need to be implemented and for whom.

Taking it Further

Write a note explaining any key strategies that you often use or any specific needs for students to stick in their diary and show new staff discretely.

Tricky subjects

'Some subjects are just more difficult for students with autism to cope with.'

There are some subjects that students with autism may find difficult to manage. This will vary from pupil to pupil but is worth bearing in mind. You need to be flexible if certain tasks within a lesson are too challenging for the student.

In making mindful adjustments, taking care with the social and communication demands on the pupil and using appropriate strategies and differentiation, most students should cope with the lessons. Some will struggle to cope with certain lessons, however, and may need extra support, withdrawal or different teaching methods to help them. Some examples are outlined below:

- **Art and design**: Sensory issues with the texture and smell of paint. They could wear gloves, use different media or work in an area slightly separated off from the rest of the class. Analysing and discussing emotions in art can also be a struggle for some. Word banks, looking at others' reviews or class mind mapping of responses to a piece could help.
- **Music**: Some children with autism are exceptional musicians, but struggle with the noise. Headphones could be worn or they may need to carry out practical sessions at a separate time.
- **Design and technology**: Handling food could be a sensory concern and fine motor skills could be problematic. It may be necessary to look at alternate recipes with ingredients the student can cope with handling. Often, tweaking one or two ingredients will work. Limit the food that

requires cutting or preparation requiring fine motor skills (though this skill may need to be taught separately). If fine motor skills are atypical, then the pupil may need support using machinery. Machinery noise could also be an issue. Headphones may help.

- **PE**: Motor skills, dislike of physical contact and difficulties working in groups can mean that group games are difficult for some. If they cannot cope with a football match, they could practice penalty shooting or write a review of the game. They may need to be given alternative work.

- **Computing**: I have many students whose talent for IT and computer programming is exceptional. They therefore often struggle or get bored having to follow the prescribed curriculum. You may need to explain to these pupils that whilst they may be 'beyond' this level in some respects, to progress they need to demonstrate the skills outlined in the curriculum and succeed in exams.

- **English:** Students with autism can have difficulty expressing and understanding emotive language. This can make evaluating literature problematic for some. Many also struggle with inference skills and so non-literal language can confuse them. Encourage them to look out for and highlight this kind of language. Where processing is an issue, reading or writing large amounts of text can be a struggle. Allow plenty of time for explanation and completion of tasks and use differentiation strategies to support their written output.

- **Science:** Some students will struggle with sensory difficulties and may need to be excused from lessons where chemical smells may be too overwhelming. The unpredictability of some experiments or simply the practical nature of some tasks may cause anxiety. Let the pupil know what to expect in advance and they may feel able to cope.

Addressing PSHE

'Teaching the PSHE curriculum is difficult, as some students are simply not interested or terrified of it!'

The Personal, Social and Health Education curriculum, is probably one of the most important for students with autism; however, often they are not equipped with the prior knowledge, social and emotional understanding to cope with the content.

Students with autism may be frightened by the thought of drugs or embarrassed by discussions about puberty and sexual relationships. Some pupils are delayed in their understanding of such matters because they may not have an interest in them, have no peer group that introduces such ideas to them, or they may feel such matters do not apply to them. They do of course matter and need to be taught, but some pupils will require teaching about personal space, body modesty and social relationships before they can cope with the content of the mainstream PSHE curriculum.

Social skills teaching help to give the student a grounding in social relationships, life skills, self-esteem support and the basics of body modesty and looking after themselves. The teaching of the PSHE curriculum may still need to be modified, but with this background they will be more likely to cope.

If the student cannot cope with the content of the lesson then they may need to be withdrawn. If this is the case, then it is important that this content is delivered in a more palatable way or at a later date. Some parents are fearful that teaching about sexual relationships or drugs and alcohol may prompt the student to experiment, but it is far safer if they are made aware of the risks and dangers.

Recording the lesson

'If a student is absent, unable to cope with a lesson or attends but cannot process information, then this strategy ensures they maximise learning and do not fall behind.'

Students with autism can struggle to process information or can become caught up in the detail of one part of an explanation, meaning they are not focusing when the lesson moves on. If you allow the lesson to be recorded, the student has the option to revisit it and fill in the gaps.

One student who was studying for his GCSEs required a lot of support with processing and breaking down the lesson content. In lessons, he would become so preoccupied with working out why an equation had to be worked through in a certain way, or fascinated by a piece of information given out, that he would become immersed in that, often then missing chunks of the lesson. As a result he became very frustrated and was at risk of falling behind. Teachers gave him one-to-one support when they could, to help him move past blocks in his thinking, but time is of course limited. We encouraged him to bring a Dictaphone into lessons and put it on the teacher's desk throughout. He could then take away the tape at the end of the lesson and listen through if he needed to fill in any gaps or consolidate learning. It worked wonders.

Video recording the lesson could also be helpful for practical activities or learning experiences out of the classroom that the pupil cannot cope with, though for day-to-day use the Dictaphone is easier to use and less distracting.

Teaching Tip

Lesson overviews, main teaching points or explanations could be given to the students on handouts or put onto memory sticks.

Bonus Idea ★

There are some good educational websites which could be used to consolidate learning, including videos of Science experiments or virtual tours of galleries. Visit www. bbc.co.uk/education/subjects/zrkw2hv and www.nationalgallery.org.uk/visiting/virtualtour/.

Get them involved

'If the student is involved in the planning and assessment process, from time to time it will enhance their learning.'

Students will be more engaged, have a clearer understanding and see a point to the lesson if they are included, at times, in the planning and assessment process. It prepares them for what is to come and consolidates learning.

This can be time consuming and may not be workable for all lessons all of the time, but, at times, this idea is a really useful way of getting the pupil thinking about the lesson content in a slightly different way. Being part of the assessment process encourages them to think about how something was achieved and can be a useful way of getting their attention and keeping them focused. Some ideas to try:

- Involve the student in decision-making. Ask them, how could we carry this out? What could we find out first that would help us do this task? Can you plan how you will complete this activity? What different ways could we do it?
- With an investigation or piece of writing, give two options of how to proceed and ask them which they think is better and why.
- Peer assessment. This may not work if too much interaction is involved but it can be useful for them to understand where others had different ideas, where they got things wrong or where they had different interpretations.
- Encourage students to think about what they have learned from the lesson that they did not know before. What went well? What did not work? What could they do differently next time?

Tackling homework

'For him, home is home and school is school and they should never overlap.'

Many students with autism struggle with the idea of homework. They may struggle to get through the day at school and associate home with calm, relaxation and discharging the stresses of the day. Homework blurs those two worlds and can cause frustration.

Consider the following when issuing homework:

- If necessary allow pupils to complete work during breaks, lunches or homework clubs.
- Provide a homework timetable showing days homework is set and days to hand in.
- Take time to explain the relevance and importance of homework.
- Set a time limit for them to work on each task.
- Liaise with parents carefully. Encourage a routine of, e.g. home, snack, 1 hour homework then relaxation or special interest time.
- Use a timer or keep a clock nearby so the child has a sense of the time passing.
- Consider the homework you set. Do they need to write in full sentences, copy out chunks of texts or write two pages? Could the skills be learned and demonstrated whilst limiting the amount of written work that is expected?
- Ensure that homework is written down clearly in their diary and the task is understood.
- Hand-in dates and expectations should be clear. If the task is 'Do a piece of writing about your hobby', you could end up with one sentence or six pages. Make sure you are specific about what you want.

Teaching Tip

Some students will benefit from a homework folder, where they can keep loose pieces of work due to be handed in.

Bonus Idea ★

Students could have memory sticks onto which the teacher can save homework and other related information.

Project and coursework

'Students need guidance with longer-term projects. It is not enough to give the brief and let them get on with it.'

Coursework can be a less stressful means of gaining marks towards a good examination grade. In theory, there is more support, plenty of time, flexibility of topic and the option to redraft. In actual fact, this can be confusing and too unstructured for some students.

Help students cope with coursework by clearly explaining expectations:

- If there are choices of topic or several questions to choose from, the student could get stuck. Guide their choice and/or offer limited options.
- Check in with the student at regular intervals to see how they are progressing and remind them of the deadline. Ensure they have noted down assignment or draft deadlines.
- Ensure they understand what is expected of them. Write down the sub headings, titles and word allowance per section; anything that will help guide them.
- If the student needs to research, ensure they know how to go about this, suggesting relevant sources of information.
- Do not presume they have absorbed everything you have said in class. They may appear to have understood, but in actual fact may only have processed half of what has been said.
- Show them examples of past work so that they know what the assignment should look like.
- If the assignment requires personal opinion, emotional response or creative writing, the student may need guidance.

Revision

'So many subjects and so many exams. These strategies help the student get organised.'

The number of subjects that students have to revise for, particularly at GCSE level, can be overwhelming. Often there can be several exams in one week and pupils can struggle to organise their time. They will need help planning their revision and staying calm.

The priority over exam period is to help the student feel in control. Create a revision timetable for them and share it with parents. Encourage parents to ensure their child takes rest breaks, exercises, eats well and has time doing the things that keep them calm.

The timetable should indicate which subjects to revise and when. Use colours to highlight key information and indicate how long to revise for. This may seem prescriptive but will help students with high levels of exam anxiety.

Methods of revision may need to be taught. Give the students examples of spider diagrams and revision cards, using sticky notes or highlighters to draw attention to key points. If you lend them relevant textbooks or worksheets to aid revision, make sure to highlight relevant pages or sections.

Ensure that students get to see and work through past papers. Revision of these is key and will help them get used to the type of questions, weighting of marks, layout and length of paper. Pupils may need help learning how to break down longer questions or how to tackle answering questions with multiple parts.

When addressing the whole class with warnings that revision is needed, be aware: the student with autism may feel this is being directed at them and become very anxious.

Taking it Further

Give out a revision tips pack outlining methods of revision, how much to do, templates, advice on when to take a break and give some reassuring words to conclude.

Preparing for exams

'Time spent preparing the student for exams is time well spent.'

Exams are completely out of the usual routine. They are sat in a different room, with a different layout and with invigilators that the student may not know. The papers and the questions within the exam are unknown and they have a limited time to get everything done. Any pressure that can be relieved in advance of or during examinations will help ensure the student works to the best of their ability.

Teaching Tip

Ensure the invigilators have information on the pupils' needs, concessions and support strategies. Also, be aware and remember students with autism may not share their anxieties with a peer group. If you notice any changes to behaviour or increased anxiety then speak with parents and support.

To begin with, the ALNCo or person responsible for exam concessions needs to apply for the support and concessions that the student is entitled to, whether that be a reader, modified papers, scribe or extra time. These entitlements need to be discussed with the pupil and parents so they know what to expect. If their peers are leaving the exam hall before them, this could be disconcerting and distracting. Prepare them for this. If a student is very easily distracted or could themselves distract others, then a separate, approved room may need to be used. Also:

- Ensure the student sees the exam room before the examinations start.
- Make the list of exam conditions and rules clear.
- Ensure the student knows how to fill in the front of the exam page and where to find the centre number.
- Identify any potential distractions or sensory concerns and take steps to remedy these.
- If possible and preferable, give the student the same seat for each exam.
- Check the chairs and desks are stable and clean.
- Ensure a clock is visible.
- If possible, have a familiar face in the room or introduce the student to the invigilator/s.

Options

'I didn't have a clue what to choose or what I was capable of – choosing my options was stressful.'

Choosing what options to take whether before the GCSE or A-level years can be a daunting experience for many students. Those with autism may struggle not only with the amount of choice and information but they may also find making such an important decision frightening since it impacts on their future.

Some students will have clear ideas about what they want to do and will not be convinced otherwise. Some will not have a clue, and will find sifting through options booklets and talking with lots of teachers on options evening overwhelming. Others will have unrealistic expectations of what they can cope with. Support the pupils and parents by breaking down the information. The following questions can guide these discussions:

- Which subjects are their strongest and weakest?
- Which subjects have a coursework element? Is this a good or bad thing for the given student?
- If the student wishes to do a vocational subject, are they aware there may be less structure and more practical work?
- What is their learning style? Some courses will require self-study, coursework, presentations – how will they cope with this?

If a student cannot decide, it may be an option to trial a full timetable of subjects but drop one at a later date if they cannot cope or dislike it. Pupils and parents may need to be reminded that if they take on a full timetable, then there will be no time for catch up work, homework or course work during the school day.

Teaching Tip

If they are struggling to decide, arrange to meet and discuss. They may feel overwhelmed or rushed in options evenings. Some students may benefit from taking one or two fewer subjects that allow some free time to study and keep on top of the work. This reduces stress and is likely to ensure higher end results.

Monitoring, tracking and paperwork

Part 8

Get informed

'Valuable information was shared through these questionnaires that really helped when preparing for transition.'

These questionnaire sheets can be used where children have complex needs or are likely to require significant support. However, they can be hugely informative and useful for all students with ALN. They help build a more in-depth picture of how the child presents, what kind of difficulties have arisen in the past, flashpoints and ways of calming the student down.

The questionnaires can go out to previous school staff, parents and with parental consent, anyone else who knows the students well.

The questions asked could include:

- What interests does your child have?
- How can you tell when he/she is anxious?
- What helps to calm him/her down?
- Are there any sensory concerns?
- What do you think your child needs to help them manage transition?

The teacher's questionnaire may ask about any social communication, speech and language or sensory difficulties. It could also ask about strategies or approaches that have worked in the school setting or anything to avoid, and whether there are any friends that the student likes to spend time with or should avoid. This could inform which classes or tutor groups the child goes into. However, staff need to be mindful that just because the student with autism would like to stay with their peer from primary school, that wish may not be reciprocated and vice-versa.

Person-centred plans

'At a glance, you can see what motivates the student and how best to support them.'

Parents, support staff and the student themselves supply the information that feeds into the creation of this information sheet. This one-page plan can be given to anyone involved with the student to engage them and help meet their needs.

For each person-centred plan, include a photo of the student so that the plan can be easily recognised. Include information about their interests and what can be used to engage them, reward them, or distract them from undesirable behaviour. In addition, there should be a section about how best to support the student and any strategies that can help if he or she is unsettled. The plan can then be decorated by the student, and/or they could include pictures of their interests. Some pupils will want more involvement in this than others. It could be written in either the first or third person, so long as it is written positively and proactively.

Ideally, send out pre-prepared sheets that parents, professionals and the student can fill in to gather information. Make sure these sheets are easy to read and don't require large amounts of writing. The opinions and comments of the student and others involved can then be triangulated and will inform the writing of the plan.

When complete, share the plan with all professionals working with the student, including on the school intranet or network.

Teaching Tip

Person-centred plans can be particularly useful at times of transition. Drawing on the knowledge of the Year 6 teacher and support staff can help form a useful plan that can be shared with secondary school staff. Similarly, the process can be repeated as needs or interests change. This could be as the student moves through the school years or as they enter sixth form or leave school.

Taking it Further

Person-centred plans can be reduced to bookmark or credit card size for the student or support staff to carry with them.

This us... ...ool serves as a reminder of different
strategies to ... ...lso as a record of strategies attempted and
their success or otherwise.

Some children with complex needs or who are experiencing difficulties settling may need to have many approaches in place to support them, or several may need to be trialled before the appropriate strategy is found. It can be difficult to recall what has been tried, when and by whom. The checklist allows professionals to see the record at a glance.

When parents ask what support has been put in place, the teacher is able to demonstrate that consistent and varied approaches have been used, and the parent can see that the school is working hard at using a range of strategies to help their child.

Print off a template for each child. Create a table and in the first column list the different strategies such as: talk time cards, laptop, Dictaphone, social story, withdrawal from lesson, amended timetable, time out cards, support for unstructured time, buddy system, named person for support, named place to go if anxious, reduced homework or time for its completion. List as many as you can think of and add to them. In adjacent columns create tick boxes for whether the strategy has been considered and then whether it was achieved, leaving space to date these. The last column is for noting the success or otherwise of the strategy.

Individual Educational Plans

'Make the IEP as user friendly as possible.'

The IEP should be a working document that teachers and support staff feed into and feed back on. The targets should be individualised and the student should be involved in and aware of the targets set so they know what they are working towards.

Students with ALN should have an IEP that identifies areas for them to work on and gives suggestions about how they might be achieved and who may help to achieve them. The targets may refer to work standards or output. I tend to try to include at least one target relating to social skills, communication or coping with change, as these are the areas that the students need the most help with and can impact on learning. Points to note when writing an IEP:

- Make the targets realistic. If they are not joining in with group work at all then their target could be to try working in a pair at first. The target can be amended when this has been achieved.
- Ensure there are supportive strategies built in. There is no point setting a target for a pupil unless thought has gone into how that target could be met and the resources or support is in place to facilitate this.
- If a student is really struggling, one or two targets may be enough.
- Targets should be regularly updated. There is no point them lingering on. Either change them, amend them or update the strategies and have another attempt.
- Encourage staff to feed back on the document and use stickers and praise. The student should see it as a working document and be pleased when their progress is recognised.

Teaching Tip

Keep the language in the IEP clear and simple. Write the targets in the first person and use bullet points avoiding excessive amounts of words. Encourage pupils to personalise their IEP, make it attractive to them by including pictures of their interests.

Bonus Idea ★

Print the targets off on a separate sheet that can travel with the student or support staff. They can give it to class teachers for direct written feedback and this highlights the targets to the teacher.

Monitoring and tracking progress

'Sometimes academic progress may not be obvious, but they are progressing in other areas.'

Monitoring academic progress and attainment is usually done very carefully in schools. However, at times there can be reasons for lack of progress and the student may be making huge leaps in their social and communication skills that could go unnoticed.

Pupils with ALN can appear to plateau with their progress, or even appear to regress. The onset of adolescence and having to manage this as well as difficulties associated with autism can mean that academic study is often the least of the pupil's concerns. Lack of progress can be concerning for pupils, parents and staff and so being able to demonstrate improvements elsewhere can be reassuring. It is helpful not only because progress in social, life and communication skills is as – if not more – important for those with autism, but also because in improving these skills, they are likely to cope better in the future with learning academically.

There are various means of recording non-academic progress. Instances of behaviour could be monitored, as well as inclusion or involvement in groups and clubs and participation in class. Establish a social communication rating scale or record where the student is reviewed termly to assess progress in these areas. This could include rating the skill between one to five for competency, which can provide an interesting overview of the development of skills over time. The tracking sheet can be made to concentrate on specific skills or a general one can be made with 20 or so questions to provide a broader overview.

Running record

'An at-a-glance record of individual pupil support and needs.'

ALNCos, tutors or class teachers could find this a useful resource, particularly for students who have a lot of external agency support or a high level of need. The construction of this file requires minimal work, but can save a great deal of time.

There are some students who go through periods when they require more support because they are struggling with behaviour or there have been changes to family circumstances and so there is more service involvement. This can result in an increase in requests for information via phone and email, more meetings and more paperwork to complete.

A running record is simply a paper file or folder with a record of incident, agency involvement and any notable outcomes. At a glance the teacher can see the date of the most recent incident or meeting, why it occurred and what outcome, referrals or strategies were implemented as a result. It provides a good overview of the package of support around a student. These are useful because they can be taken into meetings to save preparation time and information gathering and you are able to answer questions by glancing at one file rather than sifting through the more detailed files containing all student information.

I have found this useful when agencies have called to ask how the child has been presenting and what has been done to support them. I am able to quickly give dates of incidents, when I sent referrals in and what happened as a result without having to find out the information and then call back. It has saved me huge amounts of time.

> **Teaching Tip**
>
> Add an information sheet with most recent assessment scores and a copy of any recent emails, reports and the statement of educational need, and make sure all necessary information for annual reviews is included.

Annual and transition reviews

'The meetings are still comprehensive and supportive but take up much less time.'

Meetings can be worthwhile and reassuring to all involved but they can be time consuming. The ideas here could apply to most meetings and should help save some time or help it feel less rushed.

Teaching Tip

If the student is struggling in a certain lesson and you intend to withdraw them temporarily or otherwise, parental consent will need to be sought. Discuss this at the meeting and decide what the student will do during those time-out sessions.

Whether or not the child has a statement of Special Educational Needs, if they have autism then they will probably require meetings to ensure they are receiving the right level of support, that they are achieving optimally and that any required external agency support is in place. The following should help ensure all of this is covered in an efficient and effective way.

- It is important that students are involved in meetings that discuss their progress. If they do not physically attend the meetings (many do not want to) then it is important that their views are shared.
- We have created three pupil feedback forms aimed at different ability levels. These ask the pupil if they feel they are getting enough support, what they enjoy about school and what they would like to change. Less able students have a sheet where they can draw their response or just write a few words. These can be attached to the review and discussed to save writing views down.
- Make sure all relevant agencies are invited to the meeting, including careers service or college representatives to transition reviews.
- Ensure any parental feedback is received in advance so that you have the answers to questions prepared and information to hand.
- Ensure copies of the IEP, letters or any reports that need to be discussed are copied and attached in advance. This saves

Taking it Further

Use the same or similar template for School Action Plus meetings. This ensures that high standards are maintained and nothing gets missed.

doing it afterwards and they are to hand for reference.

- If you intend to refer to external agencies, have the form ready for parents to sign at the meeting.
- Scan the statement beforehand and note on the form in advance any changes or points for discussion.
- Enter any data that is definite such as assessment scores or levels of support in advance. You can then read this out rather than write it to save time.
- If there are a number of action points as a result of the meeting, read these out at the end of the meeting or email them to all in attendance to ensure all actions are followed up.

Letters and reminders

'A simple time-saving idea.'

Get organised and save time by having a file to hand with paperwork that is used throughout the school year or duplicate copies of letters and information slips.

It is important to keep parents informed. However, some students with autism can struggle with organisational skills and parents may not realise that there are letters, homework or information slips at the bottom of school bags. Save time with paperwork:

- Keep spare copies of letters to parents to hand. They can then be sent home again easily.
- Keep spare diary sheets to hand. If the school diary is forgotten, then the student can have a diary slip to take home.
- Request diaries be signed and get confirmation of receipt of reports. Students who habitually lose paperwork may benefit from having reports or important information sent in the post.
- Keep some cards to hand to send home. They could contain different kinds of information: slight concerns, homework deadlines or praise.
- Take spare copies of necessary paperwork to meetings.
- Create phone record or minutes templates to fill in when called unexpectedly or asked to attend a meeting at the last minute.
- Keep templates of letters to give to parents if they want to contact you or request support. Some parents are unable to request help. We give out simple letters saying 'Dear Mrs X, please could I arrange a meeting to see you on____'. All the parents have to do is fill in the space and sign and the contact has been made.

Safeguarding

'Getting the message across.'

How and who to tell if they have a safeguarding concern? This is one of the most important messages to get across to students. Some pupils will not remember phone numbers or procedure, so we need to ensure they have understood.

All students need to be made aware of safeguarding procedures, but it is important to be aware that those with autism in particular may struggle to communicate with others, articulate emotions or express concern, particularly when distressed. They are vulnerable. They need to be aware what constitutes a safeguarding concern, that they have the right to feel safe and secure and to whom they can go to when concerned. A script with simple language clearly showing the numbers to call is helpful:

- Safeguarding means keeping me safe.
- No one is allowed to hurt me or make me feel bad.
- No one is allowed to frighten or threaten me.
- No one is allowed to make me do something I know to be wrong.
- If I feel frightened or threatened I can talk to someone I trust.
- If someone is making me do something I think is wrong, I can talk to someone I trust.
- I can talk to a teacher or LSA I trust or a police officer.
- If I talk to someone I trust they will try to help and I will feel safe.

Teaching Tip

Give this sheet to the children or display it on walls. The text can be accompanied by visuals of happy and sad faces. I also included the number for Childline (0800 1111) and the NSPCC (also 0800 1111). Less able students may need an even simpler version of this.

Taking it Further

Print the script and paste it on to small cards with the useful contact numbers on the reverse. These can be kept in school diaries or even smaller, credit card sized versions could be kept in wallets.

Assessment for Learning

'All students can benefit from being involved in the assessment process.'

The reviewing process can help students be more aware of their learning, allow them to celebrate their success and work out where things went wrong. Students should be supported to find a reviewing process that suits them.

The process of reflecting on and reviewing work requires a certain level of understanding about learning outcomes and success criteria. Students also have to be prepared to see where they went wrong and how they could improve. Some pupils with autism will struggle with this process if they feel their way is the correct one. It is important to encourage and give suggestions, ask questions and give proactive feedback during a task. 'What do you think we will find out?' 'How else could you have chosen to complete that piece of writing?'

Less able pupils may require verbal feedback and discussion or a simple sheet for them to simply write what they felt went well and what they could improve. Simpler still, they could be asked to circle smiley or sad faces or use traffic light colours which can then be discussed. More able pupils could have review sheets at the end of a task, topic or term's work which are more detailed and designed to encourage more in-depth reflection. The sheets could have a rating scale for different aspects of the task and how well the student feels they grasped them. Alternatively a cloze procedure sheet could be used, where students have to complete the end of a sentence or fill in the blanks: 'I think this was a success because . . .' 'Next time I would do it differently by . . .'.

References

Attwood, T. (2007) *The Complete Guide to Asperger's Syndrome*. Jessica Kingsley: London

Bogdashina, O. (2003) *Sensory Perceptual Issues in Autism and Asperger Syndrome: Different Sensory Experiences - Different Perceptual Worlds*. Jessica Kingsley: London

Gray, C. (2001) *My Social Stories Book,* Jessica Kingsley: London

www.carolgraysocialstories.com/social-stories

Established in 1992 as the first childhood bereavement charity in the UK, Winston's Wish remains dedicated to supporting children after the death of a parent or sibling – find out where we've come from and where we're going.
www.winstonswish.org.uk/

The Autism Education Trust funded by the Department for Education in England has produced a range of free resources to support schools and parents in developing effective provision for children and young people on the autism spectrum.

These can be found at:
www.autismeducationtrust.org.uk

www.aettraininghubs.org.uk/wp-content/uploads/2012/05/37.1-Sensory-audit-tool-for-environments.pdf